There Has to Be a Better Way

There Has to Be a Better Way

· ·

Lessons from Former Urban Teachers

LYNNETTE MAWHINNEY AND CAROL R. RINKE

Foreword by Christopher Day

Rutgers University Press

New Brunswick, Camden, and Newark, New Jersey, and London

Library of Congress Cataloging-in-Publication Data

Names: Mawhinney, Lynnette, 1979- author. | Rinke, Carol R., author.
Title: There has to be a better way : lessons from former urban teachers / Lynnette
　　Mawhinney and Carol R. Rinke.
Description: New Brunswick, New Jersey : Rutgers University Press, [2018] | Includes
　　bibliographical references and index.
Identifiers: LCCN 2018010041 | ISBN 9780813595283 (cloth) | ISBN 9780813595276 (pbk.)
Subjects: LCSH: Education, Urban—United States. | Urban schools—United States. |
　　Teaching—Social aspects—United States.
Classification: LCC LC5131 .M355 2018 | DDC 370.9173/2—dc23 LC record available at
　　https://lccn.loc.gov/2018010041

A British Cataloging-in-Publication record for this book is available from the British Library.

♾ The paper used in this publication meets the requirements of the American National
Standard for Information Sciences—Permanence of Paper for Printed Library Materials,
ANSI Z39.48-1992.

www.rutgersuniversitypress.org

Manufactured in the United States of America

To Michele "The Rainmaker" Louis Simelane.
Sending you all the "claw love" to heaven.

Contents

Part IV   Addressing Teacher Attrition

Foreword

Michael Huberman (1993) was the first to bring a large scale, conceptually sound, empirically robust, and nuanced analysis of secondary teachers' lives by charting the different influences upon Swiss secondary school teachers during each of five phases of their professional lives. In doing so, he challenged the linear "career stage" orthodoxy that had led to the erroneous belief about the development of expertise that teachers begin as "novices," and, as experience grows, sooner or later they become "experts." Inexplicably, this linear conception continues to dominate the design of many policy-driven systems of professional development. International scholars have for many years noted that there are critical phases in teachers' lives (Sikes, Measor, and Woods 1983) and that these are influenced by psychological, life course, and work contexts (Leithwood 1990). A more recent four-year national, longitudinal, mixed methods research project in the United Kingdom (Day, Sammons, and Stobart 2007) investigated variations within and between primary and secondary teachers' lives and work during early-, middle-, and later-career phases. It found associations within and between these and their perceived and relative effectiveness in terms of students' measured progress and attainment, thus providing a more nuanced evidence-based perspective on influences on teachers' effectiveness.

Among the key quantitative and qualitative findings of that research were that there were statistically significant associations between levels of teacher commitment and student attainment; that more experienced teachers were more likely to be less committed, perhaps unsurprisingly, given the exacting nature of classroom teaching; and that teachers who taught in schools serving socioeconomically disadvantaged communities were more likely to experience health problems, more likely (particularly in secondary schools) to have to manage poor student motivation, emotions, learning engagement, and behavior on a daily basis than those in schools serving more socioeconomically advantaged communities; and that they thus required a greater capacity for emotional resilience than others. Indeed, a later reanalysis of interview data by one of the research teams found, also, a statistically significant correlation between teachers' levels of resilience and students' levels of measured attainment, in other words, the less resilient the teacher, the more likely that the students' measured progress and attainment would be below expectation, and the more resilient the teacher, the more likely that students' measured progress and attainment would be at or above expectations (Day and Gu 2013).

The contents of Lynnette Mawhinney and Carol R. Rinke's richly crafted book add to this and other research-generated knowledge of teachers' work in schools serving socioeconomically disadvantaged communities, and of the challenges they face, especially perhaps if—as with the teachers in this book— teaching is not their first-choice profession. Each chapter of the book combines academic research *about* teachers and teaching with knowledge *of* teachers and teaching through the self-reported narratives of teachers themselves who have left classroom teaching, though not always the education sector.

After a scene-setting introduction, which includes autobiographical thumbnails about the reasons why the authors themselves left classroom teaching, the book is organized thematically into four sections: the first two focus on dynamic and structural influences on teacher attrition, and the third on personal and professional issues. In the fourth section, the lessons on attrition raised in the first three are drawn together to form a series of recommendations for improving rates of teacher retention. Each chapter begins with a short overview, connecting the theme with relevant extant literature. This is followed by accounts of, for example, the reasons for choosing to become a teacher. Each chapter ends with reflective questions and recommendations for further reading. The chapters extend and deepen knowledge of key themes derived from the reported experiences of the teachers about what it is like for teachers in schools in the United States who face a range of diverse challenges associated with social and economic disadvantage by virtue of their student and community populations.

Written out of the "storied" experiences of twenty-five former secondary science and English urban teachers—who began as highly committed teachers but who left tired, burned out, and disenchanted with their abilities to "make a difference" (most before six years in the job)—each page provides "live" evidence of the highs and lows, the personal and professional trials and tribulations of these teachers. As the authors observe, many of them did not leave education but, like them, transited to a different, perhaps less emotionally hazardous, sector.

Lynnette and Carol skillfully and with great care and respect unpack the teachers' stories, revealing not only the variety of challenges that they experienced as a result, often, of policies which challenged their deepest educational ideals and values and practices, but also unsupportive colleagues and administrators, and the individual and collective effects of these on their personal lives. This makes for powerful reading, and it also serves as a powerful reminder that parents, policymakers, and school leaders alike should be concerned when teachers choose, or feel that they have no other option but to choose, to leave the place where education matters the most—the classroom.

In their selections and reframing of the stories, the authors show that teacher attrition—a theme that has become an ongoing concern for policymakers in many countries and jurisdictions—is "not a simple or hasty act based upon singular factors, but instead constitutes a long term, constructed, identity development process." This is an important finding for at least two reasons. First, it suggests that attrition as defined only as physical departure from the classroom is not a matter that affects only teachers in their early years. Second, it may suggest that there are likely to be teachers who, while remaining in schools, are surviving and coping rather than thriving and managing their work successfully, and so they may not be teaching "to their best and well" (Day 2017).

The authors' notion of teachers' lives as a "part of a career unfolding" is important also, because it places teachers as "active agents who construct their own coherent understandings of their personal and professional experiences and use those understandings to mediate career decisions"—though the book does not address the relative strength of the inner and external forces upon their professional identities.

By chance, some of the teacher participants in the study were those for whom teaching had been a second choice, and this may be seen to limit the claims that they make. However, while this may have resulted in less commitment to stay, the text does not suggest this. Indeed, although we cannot know what proportion of "first choice" teachers choose to leave teaching, for similar reasons, it is not unreasonable to suppose that some of them are also likely to have done so. The authors' choice of a snowball selection of science and English secondary teachers might also be seen to limit the wider authority of the reported findings. The results may have been different if the teachers were from elementary schools or teachers of other subjects. However, Lynnette and Carol do not claim that their twenty-five teachers are representative of the total population of teachers, nor even of the "second choice" teachers. Rather they use the testimonies of these teachers as a means of understanding and underlining that attrition is not an event but a developing process, leading to a decision to withdraw, that it is somehow associated with teachers' loss of a positive, stable sense of professional identity; and that it is the result of multiple influences that together combine to the point at which teachers make a decision to stay or leave the school and/or the profession.

Many of these teachers, like those in many other countries, cited poor administrators, disillusion with the system, constant high workloads, exhaustion, stress, contractual instabilities, and/or microaggressions as key contributors to their decision to leave. Perhaps unsurprisingly, as most are "second choice" career teachers, a substantial minority felt the pull toward joining other professions. Yet, as much other literature continues to demonstrate, it is the school principals' (administrators') qualities, actions, and relationships that make a significant difference to teachers' sense of job satisfaction, well-being, commitment, resilience, and individual and collective loyalty to the school and teaching profession: for example, in "supporting creativity and freedom, providing constructive feedback and communication, being a cheerleader . . . buffering teachers from external pressures." Sadly, as others before them have noted, the authors point to teachers' experiences of "the revolving door" of principal turnover, particularly in schools serving high-need communities, resulting in discontinuities and fragmentation of values, policies, relationships, and sense of community, not to mention the progress and achievements of many of the students in those schools.

The stories in this book have two fundamental truths about the demands of teaching on those who endeavor to teach to their best and well. First, it is well-nigh impossible if we care about the well-being and intellectual and social health of the students we teach, then it is either possible nor desirable to separate the *personal* and the *professional*. Second, commitment to teaching which is also effective requires both the head (knowledge), the hand (pedagogically and behavioral-management knowledge and skills), and the heart (emotions).

The emotional toll of "being a teacher" underpins almost everything that the authors report about these teachers' experiences of teaching. The authors cite Hochschild's (2012) work on "emotional labor," and draw a parallel with teaching in which, they claim, a part of the work is to "hide or produce emotions according to the expectations of others . . . students, administrators, colleagues and parents." They are right to point out that such emotional labor is unsustainable and almost certain to lead to stress, emotional exhaustion, and a fractured sense of (inauthentic) identity. That for these teachers their work became "emotional labor," which led to withdrawal and eventual exit, is deeply regrettable for the future students who now they will never directly influence.

It should never be forgotten that teachers are the only professionals who spend most of their working lives interacting intensively with the motivations, attitudes, and abilities of individuals and groups of learners, not all of whom may want to learn, attend school, or be taught by them. They interact with them, not only face-to-face but also indirectly, when they plan, monitor, record, and evaluate. In short, they bring their work home with them. As many of these stories demonstrate, this did not always have positive results on their personal lives.

The worry is that there are many more "first" and "second" choice teachers who are experiencing overload and stress, who are also in danger of losing their passion for teaching, yet who remain because they have no other paths to follow, do not have the courage to leave, or have, because of their deep sense of commitment, their relationships with students and colleagues, or supportive leaders, decided to stay, still determined to teach to their best and well every day with every student. It is these teachers who need the continuing support. The words of the former teachers whose experiences populate this wonderfully assembled book are relevant to both.

Christopher Day
University of Nottingham
October 2017

There Has to Be a Better Way

Introduction

● ●

Walking in through the Out Door: Professional Trajectories of Urban Teachers

Monica's passion, which could be easily mistaken for rage, made her speak so loudly and quickly on the phone that other people in the vicinity could hear her voice coming through the receiver. The most glaring of her statements was "After this school year, I'm done!" But how did Monica, a secondary science teacher for six years who had been committed to supporting her students, reach a level of frustration that made her want to walk away from it all?

It wasn't always like this. Growing up on the East Coast, Monica loved science and knew she wanted to pursue it as a career. In fact, when Monica went to college, she earned premed and secondary education/science credentials. Both programs were so intense that it took Monica five and a half years to finish her undergraduate degrees. She even took the time to get teaching certificates in multiple areas of science: biology, chemistry, and earth science.

After earning her undergraduate degrees, Monica found herself at a crossroads. She could either use her premed degree to go to medical school, or she could use her education degree to go to the classroom. Because Monica graduated around the time when the U.S. economy was facing a significant downturn, she decided teaching would be a more practical route for paying off her student debts before adding more with medical school. She accepted a student-teaching position in a large, urban district on the East Coast and fell in love. She exclaimed, "I liked the kids, I loved that they earned your respect. The people I worked with were great, so it was a good experience that left me saying okay, you know what? I can do this. I really like teaching. It's a lot of fun." After student teaching, Monica decided to continue teaching within the same urban district—this was the beginning of her career as an urban teacher.

Monica pursued teaching as if it were her mission. She really wanted her students to "realize science isn't terrible since they have preconceived 'this is going to be' terrible notions." She accomplished her goal and created lasting personal relationships with her students. Early on in her career, Monica was faced with a challenging student. Often slumped in his chair and unwilling to participate in class, Sameer just sat there. He mentally checked out of school, but Sameer still showed up every day. Although discouraged with Sameer's progress all year, Monica was determined to engage him even though it was the very last science test.

For the last test, Monica decided to create cooperative groups based on the students' class averages, so they could work together and support one another in studying for the test. She found that her students learned more by talking about the test material and engaging with it. During this group work, as Sameer kept saying, "What's the point, I was going to fail?" Monica decided to do a class lecture on the importance of trying. After the class pep talk, Sameer went to work and decided to put effort into the test. He did so well that he earned a B on his last test. At this point, Monica called Sameer out of another class to personally talk with him. She recalled, "I asked him if he knew what he thought he got, and he was like a D. I told him he got a B, and this tough kid, his eyes filled up with tears, and he gave me a hug."

The relationships she built with students like Sameer propelled Monica forward in her teaching career, keeping her on course through challenges that emerged, such as a colleague and science partner trying to sabotage her science laboratory by charging her unnecessarily for lab chemicals. Through these ups and downs, Monica just "stuck it out." And she stated, "I'll always stay in public schools because I can't handle how prissy private school is." Urban schools were where she wanted to be. But life changed.

Monica found a man and fell in love. He was from the southern part of the United States, when Monica was from the north. Eventually, Monica made the decision to move so they could be together and get married. Her husband is a teacher in a public school, but with the move, the only available position Monica found was teaching biology and physiology at a private school. Begrudgingly, she took the position, along with a significant pay cut, transitioning her from an urban teacher to a school for privileged children. This was a big change from having students on probation to ones who drove fancy cars and had parents paying $20,000 for high school tuition.

Six years into her career, Monica reached her saturation point. First were the financial strains from the low wages she took from the pay cut. Her inability to save any money or buy a home at her age really started to wear her down. The added frustrations of dealing with chronic work overload, coupled with the entitled attitudes of the privileged students she taught, made for a perfect storm. Monica was planning her exit, but she was not the first to leave. She explained: "Another friend of mine quit two years ago. She's been working on her PhD in education for a year. People that are really good teachers and intelligent are getting out of it to either change the policies, or they just love it so much that they can bypass the ones that don't see the value in education."

Monica left without a clear transition plan. She decided to pursue two new career directions at the same time. Monica applied to a two-year, full-time medical program in order to become a physician's assistant, with the hope of working toward surgery. Like teaching, surgery is different every day, which was appealing, as Monica hates monotony. But if this plan did not work out, Monica was also determined to change the educational system. She shared, "If I don't go to PA school I'm going to go to graduate school for either education policy or advancement because so much needs to change. But even if I don't get to pursue science further I'm going to do something higher up in education that involves policy." And with that decision, Monica (a pseudonym) started to slowly pack up her high school classroom; she was itching to get out of the teaching profession.

The Effects of Teacher Attrition

Monica's story is a common one. In many countries around the world, teachers are closing the classroom door, never to return. High rates of teacher attrition pose a pressing problem, resulting in decreased achievement for students, high financial costs for schools, and deprofessionalization for teachers (Grissmer et al. 2000; Ingersoll and Merrill 2012; Carroll 2007). In the United States, estimates vary, but analyses of the National Schools and Staffing Survey show that between 17 and 46 percent of new teachers leave the classroom within their first five years (Gray and Taie 2015; Ingersoll 2003), and this is more complicated within urban school districts, where 50 percent of teachers, on average, leave within three years (Ingersoll 2003).

Not only are these rates of attrition far higher than in equivalent professions such as nursing (Ingersoll and Merrill 2012), but they also negatively impact students, schools, and teachers. Teacher expertise increases over time; thus teacher attrition results in a less experienced workforce that is harmful to student achievement and may have a disruptive effect schoolwide (Henry, Fortner, and Bastian 2012; Ronfeldt, Loeb, and Wyckoff 2013). Recent calculations have also estimated the annual cost of teacher turnover in the United States to be $7.34 billion (Carroll 2007). Further, some have argued that high rates of teacher attrition are undermining years of professionalization, changing the image of teaching from "highly complex work, requiring specialized knowledge and skills" (Ingersoll and Merrill 2012, 19) toward a more technical model.

The irony of teacher attrition is that in the United States, teachers have to go through a long and arduous process just to become certified; teacher education is the only college major requiring a professional certification test for completion of the degree (Petchauer 2012). To gain acceptance into a teaching program, prospective teachers need to test into the major with a basic skills exam. The basic skills exam is a major roadblock for many prospective teachers, especially prospective teachers of color (Bennett, McWhorter, and Kuykendall 2006; Mawhinney 2014; Nettles et al. 2011). If the prospective teachers are able to get through this first "hoop," they still have a second series of state-level professional examinations to pass in order to complete a successful student teaching experience. There is now a movement in many states to mandate high-stakes performance examinations (e.g., edTPA) that require the completion of a significant number of hours (both for the student and the cooperating teacher) as well as high financial costs payable to private testing companies (averaging $300 per test). After successfully completing these multiple and often-expensive obstacles to become a teacher, almost half of these teachers do not stay past five years.

On the other hand, the research shows that most teachers do not reach their full skill level in teaching until year seven (Carroll and Foster 2010). If we hold this to be true, most teachers are leaving prior to mastering the profession, and many students have the opportunity to learn only from novice teachers. Year after year of novice teaching has been shown to negatively impact student achievement (Henry, Fortner, and Bastian 2012; Ronfeldt, Loeb, and Wyckoff 2013). Essentially, these teachers are walking in through the out door. The profession of teaching has effectively transformed into a temporary occupation.

Teaching: The Starter Career

Extant research suggests that the current teaching profession in the United States operates within an exploratory context, in which teaching is viewed by some as only a temporary occupation. The research also indicates that teachers' careers are shaped by both intrinsic and extrinsic factors. Although teaching in the United States was originally constructed as a temporary occupation, starting in the 1950s, it underwent an extended period of professionalization (Rury 1989). More recently, researchers have noted that the current generation of teachers, especially women and teachers of color, has far greater economic and professional opportunities available to them outside the field of education than earlier generations enjoyed (Johnson 2007). This change, combined with a larger trend toward multidimensional careers (Dwyer and Wyn 2007), a prolonged transition from education to work (Roberts, Clark, and Wallace 1994), and the proliferation of alternative routes into the classroom (Zeichner and Conklin 2009), has resulted, for many, in a recasting of teaching as a temporary career exploration rather than a long-term professional commitment. Current educational forces argue for a reconceptualization of teachers' career development so that it is understood as a longitudinally constructed process.

Several studies have looked at teachers' careers within the current exploratory context in the United States and around the world. These studies have found that teachers today fall into a number of categories, which range in terms of commitment and intended longevity. In the United States, Peske and colleagues (2001) distinguished between teachers with contributing and exploring orientations. Likewise, in the United Kingdom, Smethem (2007) identified three types of teachers, which she terms "classroom," "career," and "portfolio" teachers, who are differentiated by their goals and intentions. In Australia, Watt and Richardson (2008) found a similar dynamic, classifying teachers as highly engaged "persisters," highly engaged "switchers," and lower engaged "desisters." Finally, among urban educators in the United States, Freedman and Appleman (2008) categorized teachers as "traditional stayers," "movers" remaining in urban education, and "leavers." Taken together, these typologies suggest that today's exploratory context opens up the traditional teaching-career ladder into a number of diverse pathways that vary with respect to commitment, duration, and engagement in classroom-based work.

Intrinsic and Extrinsic Factors

Drilling down from the societal to the individual teacher perspective, research has indicated that both intrinsic and extrinsic motivators influence teachers' career decisions. Lortie (1975) originally recognized the priority of psychic rewards to teachers, while others have noted that passion and mission are more influential in the work lives of teachers than in the work lives of other professionals (Goldstein 2014). The majority of teachers choose teaching because of its social usefulness (Smulyan 2004; Weiner 1990), and they see teaching as not just a job, but as a reflection of their identity (O'Brien and Schillaci 2002). These intrinsic motivators have also been shown to shape teachers' lifelong career trajectories as well as their levels of satisfaction with the profession (Scott, Stone, and Dinham 2001). In her study of long-serving teachers in high-poverty schools in the United Kingdom, McIntyre (2010) found that teachers' emotional connection to their workplace was central to their longevity. Likewise, Nieto's (2001, 2003) work with U.S. teachers found that personal biographies, connections to students, and intellectual work sustained them in the profession over time. However, mission can also precipitate teachers to leave classroom teaching; Santoro (2011) identified a group of principled leavers who chose to leave teaching because the practices of schooling contradicted their core ethical beliefs.

Alongside the research on intrinsic motivators stands a body of literature on the influence of extrinsic factors on teachers' careers. Dinham and Scott

(1998, 2000), in their international Teacher 2000 Project, identified three domains relevant to teacher satisfaction: largely satisfying intrinsic factors, more varying school-based factors, and largely dissatisfying extrinsic factors. Barber and Mourshed (2007), in their international comparison of high-performing educational systems, found that the high status of teaching in certain countries was vital in attracting individuals to the profession. Conversely, Snodgrass (2010) found that the low status of teaching in the United States deterred high-achieving women from entering the field. Along with status, salary has also been established as influential to teachers' careers. Imazeki (2002) found that increases in overall salaries and maximum district salaries reduced teacher attrition from one U.S. state, and Gray and Taie (2015) found that nationally, U.S. teachers with higher starting salaries were less likely to leave the profession. Working conditions also matter greatly to teachers' satisfaction and intended retention, with conditions ranging from physical facilities (Buckley, Schneider, and Shang 2005), school leadership (Ladd, 2011), support and collaboration (Johnson, Kraft, and Papay 2012), to autonomy and decision making (DeAngelis and Presley 2011).

The changing dynamics of the teaching profession, coupled with the influence of intrinsic and extrinsic factors on teachers' career pathways, led us to ask: Where are the voices of these former teachers? Why are they choosing to leave?

Where Are They? Locating the Missing Voices of Teacher Leavers

The voices of former teachers are merely a whisper in the literature. A wealth of research has attended to the dynamics of teacher attrition in the United States and worldwide (e.g., Macdonald 1999; Quartz et al. 2008; Rinke 2008, 2009, 2014; Smethem 2007). However, much of that research focuses on practicing teachers' projected attrition. Teachers who have voluntarily left classroom teaching prior to retirement (hereafter termed "teacher leavers") are a notoriously difficult group to identify and study. As many teacher leavers are no longer associated with schools or school districts, they frequently disappear from the research literature after they leave the formal institutions of education.

Analyses that do exist indicate that teachers typically leave either for personal or contextual reasons (Goldring, Taie, and Riddles 2014; Patterson, Roehrig, and Luft 2003), although some leave because they feel they can no longer uphold their principles within the school setting (Santoro 2011). One study, which included teacher leavers as well as retirees, indicates that former teachers are more satisfied with their salary, work/life balance, professional prestige, and ability to make a difference outside the classroom (Goldring, Taie, and Riddles 2014). We also have seen that some teacher leavers struggle to transition into new careers (Rinke 2013) and that 5.8 percent of teacher leavers remain unemployed (Goldring, Taie, and Riddles 2014).

There are a few large-scale, survey studies around teacher leavers using the National Center for Educational Statistics (NCES) data sets, although one pitfall of this approach is that the data sets include retirees. Fowler and Mittapalli (2006) tried to determine the new jobs of teacher leavers, Hancock (2016) used the data sets to explore music teachers' reasons for leaving, and You and Conley (2015) looked at intentions to leave. These quantitative approaches are a start to understanding teacher leavers through broad descriptors (e.g., work environment, job satisfaction, etc.), but nuanced studies of the storied experiences of teacher leavers are missing.

Schaefer, Downey, and Clandinin (2014) point out that the important and compelling experiences of teacher leavers are not addressed in the literature. They are some of the few researchers who have explicitly captured the voices of teacher leavers. In their interviews of four teacher leavers, they also identified why teacher leavers might not want to share their stories in a study: "Teachers who leave also know that most often, if they tell these complex, layered stories, they run the risk of being seen as deficit, as selfish, as not able to 'hack it,' as 'not swimming but sinking,' Better to tell the safe stories of less risk" (Schaefer, Downey, and Clandinin 2014, 24). In essence, teacher leavers create "cover stories to leave by." For example, one of the study's participants, Ali, would say when asked that she left teaching to "be a mom" or attend "graduate school." But, as the researchers explained, "While both are possible ways to tell her stories, they are also cover stories that silence the struggles and bumping places she experienced between composing narratively coherent stories to live by on her personal and professional knowledge landscapes. Her silence about the harder to tell more complex stories could have disrupted the professional knowledge landscape of schools" (Schaefer, Downey, and Clandinin 2014, 23). Thus, these storied experiences of teacher leavers provide a rich understanding about the decisions behind leaving that need to be heard.

This book attempts to fill this void in the literature. We spent a year tracking down as many teacher leavers as we could find across the United States in order to capture their voices and experiences. We sought to understand how a group of teacher leavers experienced their careers before, during, and after classroom teaching. We specifically focused on the highest-need areas, including former teachers from urban schools, and science and English classrooms, while also striving for national representation.

We utilized life history interviews (Atkinson 1998) to inquire about teacher leavers' prior schooling, entry into teaching, classroom experiences, transition from teaching, and current career paths. We selected the life history method because of its emphasis on integrating the personal with the professional in constructing coherent narratives across the life span of teacher leavers (Goodson and Sikes 2001). Atkinson (1998) notes that life history interviews inform "how . . . individuals have found their centers through their chosen profession . . . [and] illustrate the primacy . . . of the quest for life's meaning" (16–17). We conducted life history interviews in the interpretivist tradition, soliciting and privileging the meaning teacher leavers constructed of their own lives and experiences (Denzin and Lincoln 2011).

The Teacher Leavers

Twenty-five teacher leavers were selected from multiple geographic regions of the United States, including the East, South, Midwest, and West. Trying to locate teacher leavers was an arduous and difficult task. Once teachers are out of the educational networks, they are "off the radar," and this is often why their voices have gone missing in the literature. In an effort to focus on one hard-to-staff group, we targeted former teachers of secondary science. Research indicates that secondary science teachers are more likely to leave the profession than other teachers because of their higher status (Hoyle 2001), higher dissatisfaction (Ingersoll 2003), and higher opportunity cost for teaching (Murnane and Olsen 1990). We also focused on one segment of the teaching population that is considered the most overworked—English language arts teachers. Because they must deal with the additional paperwork created by grading essays and the like, they have the most significant workload of all the secondary specializations, and we wanted to see if this workload played a role in former English language arts teachers' decisions to leave the profession (Hancock and Scherff 2010).

In order to locate teacher leavers, we used selective purposive sampling (Patton 1990) to identify secondary science and English teacher leavers who voluntarily left the profession between the years 2004 and 2014, a range reflective of current societal dynamics. We selected subject-area groups because of the discipline-specific experiences of educators (Hancock and Scherff 2010; Helms 1998). When teacher leavers were no longer associated with formal educational institutions, we solicited participation via a variety of electronic and social network platforms, including email, listservs, Facebook, and LinkedIn; snowball sampling was also used.

In addition to aiming for a geographically diverse representation of participants, we also selected for a range of characteristics, including gender, race and ethnicity, years of classroom experience, teacher preparation route, school context, and current professional field (Table 1.1).

Our participants generally reflected the predominantly white and female U.S. teaching force (Papay 2007). Our participants were 84 percent female and 16 percent male, 68 percent white, 12 percent black, 4 percent Asian, and 16 percent came from multiple backgrounds. Among these teacher leavers, 56 percent pursued traditional, university-based teacher preparation, whereas

Table I.1

Participant Overview

Participant	Gender	Race / ethnicity	Teacher prep.	Years taught	Subject taught	Current field
Abigail	F	Black	Master's	2	English/special ed.	African dance school Owner/higher education
Alice	F	Asian	Undergrad	5	Science	Business
Amber	F	White	Master's	14	English	Higher education
Andrew	M	White	Alternative	10	Science	Education administration
Anita	F	White	Undergrad	17	Science/Special Ed.	Community outreach education
Ayana	F	Black	Alternative	3	Science	Community education administrator
Beatrice	F	Asian/White	Master's	2	Science	Graduate school (education)
Catherine	F	White	Alternative	4	Science	Medicine
Erika	F	White	Master's	3	English	Graduate school (education)
Jennifer	F	Black	Alternative	14	Science	Higher education
Jeremy	M	White	Master's	5	Science	Higher education
Jordan	F	White	Alternative	9	Science	Technology
Kaitlin	F	White	Alternative	2	Special Ed.	Politics
Kelsey	F	White	Master's	5	Science	Caregiver
Lily	F	White	Alternative	6	English & Science/Special Ed.	Graduate school (education)
Liana	F	White	Master's	5	Science	Educational policy and evaluation
Lora	F	Black/Asian	Alternative	6	English	Graduate school (education)
Mason	M	White	Undergrad	15	Science	Pastor
Miles	M	White	Master's	23	Science	Community education Administrator/graduate school (education)
Monica	F	White	Undergrad	6	Science	Medicine
Nina	F	Asian/White	Alternative	4	Science	Medicine
Patricia	F	White	Alternative	2	Science	Graduate school (science)
Sasha	F	Arab/White	Undergrad	3	English	Higher hducation
Sidney	F	White	Master's	6	English	Program evaluation/graduate school (education)
Susan	F	White	Alternative	6	English	Nonprofit

44 percent pursued alternative certification routes. They ranged from having 2 to 23 years of classroom teaching experience, with an average of 7.08 years. Currently, 60 percent remain in nonteaching roles in education or education-related fields (e.g., community education), whereas the other 40 percent are engaged in fields as diverse as medicine, science, religion, government, and family caregiving.

Defining "Urban"

The twenty-five teacher leavers came from fourteen different states across the United States. The breadth of urban teacher voices spans some of the largest metropolitan school districts in the country to smaller urban districts. The definition of "urban" is often neglected in educational research (Irby 2015; Milner 2012). In an attempt to more clearly operationalize urban education research, we use Milner's (2012) typology of urban education. Participating teacher leavers taught, for the majority of their teaching careers, in two main types of schools in the typology: (1) *urban intensive schools*, or schools located in large metropolitan areas, and (2) *urban emergent schools*, or schools located in cities with populations smaller than one million people. Milner explains that the third school in the typology, *urban characteristic schools*, are "not located in big cities but may be beginning to experience increases in challenges that are sometimes associated with urban context such as an increase in English language learners in a community. These schools may be located in what might be considered rural or even suburban areas" (560). Three of our participants were in urban-characteristics schools, one in a rural district, and two in a suburban district. This investigation into the life experiences of former urban teachers attends to the full professional life cycle of educators, expanding on existing work that captures the life cycle of teachers within a school setting (e.g., Day and Gu 2010; Huberman 1989) and offering insights for constructing career pathways that reflect the realities of today's teacher workforce and their career development.

Teachers' Careers as Constructed Process

In contrast to some prior research that identified factors that make teachers at lower or higher risk for attrition (e.g., Dworkin 1980; Hancock and Scherff 2010), our study built on a theoretical framework capturing the life experiences and career development processes of teacher leavers. This approach is grounded in a social constructivist and life-design framework that "envisions 'life trajectories' in which individuals progressively design and build their own lives, including their work careers" (Savickas et al. 2009, 241). It also reveals our underlying assumption that teacher attrition is not a simple or hasty act based on singular factors, but instead constitutes a long-term, constructed, identity-development process (Savickas 2012). Flores and Day (2006) note that teachers' personal and professional histories mediate their professional identities, and Clandinin et al. (2015) build on that notion to connect the "identity making process" (3) to teachers' career trajectories.

We grounded this study on an understanding that teacher career development is an ongoing negotiation between life experiences and workplace contexts, with an eye to establishing a sense of success within the profession (Rinke 2014). We also recognized that, as part of this negotiation, teachers establish narrative coherence within their career trajectories (Schaefer, Downey, and Clandinin 2014). In this study, we built on this framework by capturing teachers' career pathways in their own voices and valuing not only their jobs but also their lives as part of a career unfolding (Tiedeman and Miller-Tiedeman 1985). We saw teachers not as passive players subjected to external influences, but as active agents who construct their own coherent understandings of their personal and professional experiences and use those understandings to mediate career decisions.

We also complicated the phenomenon of teacher attrition by noting that it is not the either-or proposition of staying or leaving. Instead, we understood teacher career development as having three primary trajectories: remaining a classroom teacher, shifting into an education-related field, and leaving education altogether (Ingersoll and Perda 2010). A growing accumulation of research suggests that a substantial number of teachers leave the classroom but remain connected to the field of education in both personal and professional ways (e.g., Donaldson et al. 2008; Margolis 2008; Quartz et al. 2008). Our research conceptualized teacher leavers as individuals who have both shifted out of classroom teaching as well as left the field of education altogether.

We Were Teacher Leavers Too

As former urban classroom teachers who transitioned into teacher education faculty, we based this inquiry on our own personal experiences as well as prior research on the longitudinal career trajectories of educators. We both entered classroom teaching through traditional preparation routes in the late 1990s, a time of renewed national interest in the field of education, a larger societal force that likely influenced our career construction. Although we encountered frustrations and rewards while working at multiple school sites, we both left classroom teaching for doctoral programs. We also continually aimed to build rapport with our participants during the interviews by sharing our own related life experiences and generating a form of reciprocity that Zigo (2001) refers to as collaboration in labor. We recognize that this reciprocity is inherently limited (Rinke and Mawhinney 2014); nonetheless, we endeavored to provide emotional support to teachers who were still struggling with the emotional challenges of the career construction process.

Because we were explicit with our participants about our stories, we feel it is important to be just as explicit with our readers. We acknowledge that our own life experiences provide a lens for how we understood the interview data. This is why we take the time to outline our stories here.

Lynnette's Story

I remember the first time I realized I was a teacher leaver. It was 2007, and I was sitting on the floor of my bedroom, papers and notes scattered everywhere, as I was talking on the phone with Carol. We were brainstorming and figuring out the details of our first joint research project, years before we started to look at teacher leavers. While brainstorming, Carol mentioned, "You know, it would be interesting to find out about teachers that left." I replied, "Yeah, right? I mean, . . ." and then it hit me, like a ton of bricks. It hit so hard, that's why this memory is so clear in my head. As I continued with my jaw slightly dropped, I said, "because we're teacher leavers, aren't we?" Carol confirmed it on the other line, and a jolt of guilt ran through my body.

Why was this such a shock to me? I left my high school English classroom in Philadelphia four years prior to this discussion. Shouldn't I have known that I was a leaver? Wouldn't that be obvious? But, as Schaefer, Downey, and Clandinin (2014) explained, I was always using my cover story. My cover story was that I was going to graduate school to get my PhD. Sure, this was true. Some of my high school students were upset that I was leaving, but others were excited that they now knew someone, especially a Black woman who looked like them, getting their "Playa Hater Degree." I would explain that this move to graduate school would make me a better teacher—which was also true. But that wasn't the real depth of the story; all of this was a cover story for my students, and I came to discover I did not want to admit that the job defeated me.

Here is the real story. I was an outlier compared to our research participants, as I always wanted to teach. I went into teacher education as an undergraduate and never changed my major. Teaching is really where my heart was. I loved my job teaching. After all these years, my students still have a special place in my heart and life. My relationships with them continued long after I left—from graduations to baby showers. Even after I finished my PhD, I worked at a Historically Black University (HBCU) that some of my former high school students also attended, and the connection of teaching and relationship building continued to grow.

But . . . I was at war with the administration at the public charter school where I taught. The head of the school (we'll call her Ms. Joyless) continually bullied the teachers. She would enforce numerous unethical practices, and because we had no union, teachers were often fired for trying to resist her or even for publicly attempting to blow the whistle on her. Ms. Joyless and I would battle, I often resisted, and I would get away with it, as my students often scored high on the standardized tests. In short, my students made her and the school look good.

During my last year of teaching, it all came to a head. She called me to her office. Her niece was in my advisory (i.e., homeroom), and I was responsible for her report card. Her niece, a super smart girl who lacked motivation, got a C in my English class, a C in science class, and a C in her law-class elective, and the rest of her grades were A's. Ms. Joyless informed me in a very loud and stern voice—after using many "choice words" in this meeting—that "My niece is an honor roll student. You need to change these grades, or you need to rethink if you want to continue working here." This was a direct threat—change the grades or I would be fired. I talked with the science and law teachers, and they advised me to automatically change their grades for Ms. Joyless's niece to an A. Interestingly, the law teacher randomly quit on the spot approximately two months after this incident. But unlike the science and law teachers, I was on the fence about changing the grade in my class. What was my student going to learn from this experience? Is standing up for this reason worth being out of a job? The decision put so much stress on me that I was stuck in bed with a high fever for two days. The one decision I did make was that I was not going to come back to teaching at that school after the academic year was done. Graduate school was a quick escape. It gave me a chance to catch my breath from (what felt like) a battered soul, while giving me time to figure out my game plan.

All through graduate school, I always envisioned myself going back to the high school classroom. But as I got more experience teaching undergraduate courses, I realized my undergraduate students were the same students with the same needs, but I did not have "administration" breathing down my neck. The excessive growth of standardized tests in the K–12 spectrum was just beginning, and I knew my inherent resistance to teaching to the test would become a harder battle to fight. I decided to stay in higher education. I felt I could make a bigger difference working with prospective urban teachers, and my effectiveness would be more widespread. Instead of influencing the one hundred students in my high school classroom each year, I could influence the one hundred preservice teachers I have each semester, and they, in turn, would influence their own classrooms of one hundred students. I still see myself and identify as a teacher, but the reality is I am a teacher leaver who is still trying to emotionally recover from that very delayed realization.

Carol's Story

Like many of the teachers we interviewed, I did not grow up wanting to be a teacher. My mother was actually a teacher leaver herself, fleeing what she described as the chaos of a seventh-grade Spanish classroom for the quiet of database work. As I grew up, I really wasn't sure what I wanted to do. I was interested in nature, so I studied biology in college and thought I would go into some form of environmental protection. One summer spent doing environmental protection work in an office job showed me that was not the right path for me. I wanted something active and engaging, plus I had enjoyed my summers working with children as a camp counselor. Based on these informal experiences, I decided to try out teaching and enrolled in a master's certification program in secondary biology. Perhaps, like many young people entering the workforce for the first time, I had very little understanding of what it meant to pursue a career as a teacher.

My first teaching job involved teaching science and math at an alternative school in New York City. Having grown up in a largely white suburban community, I had little concept of what it meant to be a white teacher in a predominantly Black and Hispanic community. Very little in my preparation had helped me to see the dynamics of race and power in my interactions with students. It actually wasn't until I was in my PhD program a few years later that I was able to unpack some of those interactions with students and see how much I had missed. I am not sure that I was truly a "teacher" to my students that first year, as I spent most of my time frantically trying to figure out what I was going to do the very next day. While I developed valuable one-on-one relationships with students, I'm not sure that I reached a point where I could merge relationship, content, and pedagogy, as veteran educators do so seamlessly.

The challenges of my first year in the classroom gradually diminished as I gained more experience. Getting a fresh start with a new group of students in my second year allowed me to build on what I had learned. By my third year in the classroom, I had become a model for new teachers at my school, who were brought by my classroom to observe how I fostered dialogue and sustained positive relationships with students while maintaining high expectations. I learned a bit more about biology as well, finally solidifying my understanding of photosynthesis as well as how to teach it. I felt like I was finally hitting my stride as a teacher.

So imagine how surprised I was to find that, after overcoming the challenges of the first few years in the classroom, I was not thrilled with my chosen career. Like many teacher leavers we interviewed, it wasn't that I didn't enjoy the teaching or the students. I got a lot of joy from those relationships and interactions. What I didn't like was teaching all day every day. Perhaps like my mother, I found myself to be more of an introvert than I had realized. I loved my classes first period, second period . . . but by the end of the day, I was tired and bored. One snowy day, I decided to begin looking into alternatives that would allow me to keep teaching, but also offer me the opportunity to think, write, and reflect. I made the decision to apply to graduate school for my PhD.

Even after making the decision to become a teacher leaver, my career did not follow a straight path. At first, I decided to pursue part-time graduate work in biology, enrolling in night classes at a local institution. That first semester,

I spent every second of my spring break working on a project on metabolic adaptations that left me feeling exhausted, so I decided that full-time graduate work might be a better fit. I was also advised to switch from the sciences to science education and enrolled in a doctoral program at a larger, land-grant university. Here again, my path was not clear. After one year in science education, I realized that I was more interested in teacher development than curriculum and instruction and switched within the institution to a teacher preparation doctoral program. I had finally found my academic home, where I learned how to better prepare others for the work I had been doing.

Overview of Chapters

The book is divided into four major sections. Part I, "The Dynamics of Teacher Attrition," which includes chapter 1, "Push and Pull in Career Development," provides an overview of the twenty-five teacher leavers and how they constructed their own career pathways through an ongoing negotiation between personal and professional factors. The chapter discusses how the former teachers' career pathways are shaped by dynamics of push and pull in *choosing teaching*, in *leaving teaching*, and around *teachers' passions*.

Part II, "Structural Factors in Teacher Attrition," which contains three chapters, addresses the systematic features of education that influence teacher attrition. Chapter 2, "The Struggle Is Real: Administrators, Teachers, and the System," explores the relationship between administrators and teachers and systemic pressures they tend to face. Although administrators and teachers are often thought to work together as an effective team—and we discuss examples of this with the teacher leavers' stories—we found the fractures in these team structures to be a major catalyst for teachers' departures. This chapter, along with all the remaining chapters, provides positive and actionable goals for both school administrators and teacher educators.

While chapter 2 discusses the professional struggles behind teachers' decisions to leave, chapter 3, "Wading through the Waters: Exhaustion, Stress, and Disillusionment with Teaching," looks at the emotionality behind the decision to leave. The former teachers describe succumbing to the fatigue of the workload, the overbearing expectations of the job, and disillusionment of teaching within "broken" school systems. This chapter wades through the emotional component that contributed to the participants' decision to leave, while also addressing implications that emerged from these strained teacher-administrator relationships, including the fundamental importance of how to manage stress and reduce workloads. Chapter 4, "Where Has All the Job Security Gone?" reveals how teaching, once considered to be a stable profession, has shifted over the years. This chapter discusses the particulars of three teacher leavers and the impact and frustration created from job insecurity. It concludes with a discussion of how to value teachers' expertise while supporting them through more consistent approaches to change.

Part III, "The Personal and the Professional in Teacher Attrition," contains three chapters that address the interaction of different facets of teacher identity with the teaching profession. Chapter 5, "You Don't Fit Here: Teachers of Color Coping with Racial Microaggressions in Schools," reports on the microaggressions experienced by teachers of color during their teacher training and in the workplace and their immediate and long-term impacts. It is followed by recommendations for how administrators and teacher educators can provide a safe space to promote dialogue around race. Chapter 6, "Negotiating Gendered and Cultural Expectations on a Teacher's Salary: The Mediating Role of Identity," focuses on the salience of salary in shaping teachers' career decisions, despite social norms emphasizing intrinsic over extrinsic factors. Moreover, we found that teachers' perceptions of salary were mediated by both gendered and cultural expectations, such that teachers interpreted their income through a lens of identity and reached career decisions through an identity-making process. The chapter discusses how to prioritize salary and invest in identity. Chapter 7, "I Just Feel So Guilty: The Role of Emotions in Leaving," explores the emotions around leaving teaching that endure years after the fact. Some teachers continue to struggle with guilt around their decision to leave, but they continue to be urban education advocates outside of the classroom. The chapter concludes with a dialogue around teacher resiliency and emotional recognition.

In Part IV, "Addressing Teacher Attrition," chapter 8, "Closing the Revolving Door: Teacher Leavers' Final Lesson for the Profession," widens the lens and identifies strategies for promoting meaningful teacher retention. In this concluding chapter we discuss the reframing of mission-driven teaching to mission-guided teaching within teacher education and how administrations can use sabbaticals as an effective tool for maintaining teacher retention in schools. We also recommend taking a wider view of teaching in comparison with other professions to foster mutual learning and growth.

Part I

The Dynamics of
Teacher Attrition

●●●●●●●●●●●●●●●●●●●●●●

1

Push and Pull in
Career Development

· ·

The life history experiences of these twenty-five teacher leavers are shaped by an ongoing dynamic of *push and pull* in teachers' career paths. Much previous research has looked at only one of these aspects at a time—that is, factors that pull teachers to the classroom (e.g., Nieto 2003; O'Brien and Schillaci 2002) *or* factors that push teachers out of the classroom (e.g., Gray and Taie 2015; Ladd 2011). In either case, the lens traditionally has focused on features of education that influence teachers' decisions. Our data suggest that these teacher leavers instead negotiated a simultaneous push *and* pull in which they balanced features of teaching with features of other positions and fields. This simultaneous push-and-pull dynamic appeared repeatedly in the teacher leavers' narratives. This essential reframing of how teachers negotiate their career pathways highlights the importance of looking not only at features of education that push and pull teachers' careers, but also the overarching societal context in which education operates, including the direct competition for human capital (Hargreaves and Fullan 2012).

This chapter provides an overview of all the teacher leavers and the dynamic movement within their careers. Specifically, we discuss how the teacher leavers were pushed and pulled into choosing teaching, pushed and pulled into leaving teaching, and pushed and pulled around their passions. We also highlight some of the structural as well as personal factors influencing teachers' decisions as they designed their own career paths. This holistic viewpoint establishes the framework for understanding the complexities of teacher leavers' choices in the subsequent chapters.

Push and Pull in Choosing Teaching

In looking across the career pathways of these teacher leavers (see table 1.1), one of the most striking patterns that emerges is that all but two of the twenty-five teacher leavers, including those who earned undergraduate degrees in education, initially intended to enter other fields, from anthropology to policy to theater. Some took those initial intentions more seriously and further than others, but with only two exceptions, all these teacher leavers entered college without plans to pursue teaching. Even those teacher leavers who completed undergraduate teacher certification programs had other plans in mind: Monica completed a teacher certification along with a premedical program; Anita thought she was going to be a translator before going into bilingual education; Sasha mentioned taking education courses because she thought they would be "easy passes"; and Mason transferred midway from physical therapy to teaching. Alicia, one of two teacher leavers who entered college intending to become a teacher, said she was pushed by her parents into a well-recognized and respected field for women.

Most of the participants, rather than planning to pursue teaching, aspired toward high-status, traditional professions such as medicine, law, or academia. In fact, the majority of the teacher leavers had clear graduate-school plans, with seven participants aspiring to, applying, and at times even beginning doctoral programs. Another six were heading toward medical school, two were considering law school, and three were interested in government or community-based work. Although some of this dynamic may stem simply from the high visibility of these traditional professions, it is at least worthwhile considering that the high status and prestige of these fields attracted them to the fields as well (Hoyle 2001). In this way, teaching emerged as a "second choice" for these twenty-five teacher leavers.

The majority of participants explained they were drawn to teaching at some point later in their career development because of the opportunity to make a difference or influence students. Fifteen out of the twenty-five mentioned these goals—a common theme for motivation in the teaching literature (e.g., Watt et al. 2012). For Patricia, who held a strong interest in science policy, teaching offered the opportunity to shape the views of the next generation. She explained, "You're educating future citizens to think critically about issues like climate change, pollution or environmental justice." Mason, who taught chemistry and coached football, noted, "I went into education to help kids lead healthy, positive, productive lives." And Lora says she was greatly influenced by the "image of Black and brown kids not having access to a college education."

Table 1.1
Participant Career Overview

Participant	Original career direction	Pathway into teaching (personal)	Pathway into teaching (professional)	Pathway out of teaching (personal)	Pathway out of teaching (professional)
Abigail	Law	Personality fit	Recognized career	Disillusion	Flexibility and support
Alicia	Education	Unsure career direction	Recognized career	Exhaustion and salary	Corporate recruiting
Amber	English	Informal teaching	Make a difference	Continue learning	Broaden influence
Andrew	Foreign policy	Dissatisfaction	Make a difference	Salary	Financial security
Anita	Translation	Felt right	Recognized career	Continue learning	Broaden influence
Ayana	Theater	Informal teaching	Influence students	Exhaustion	Arts
Beatrice	Science	Less solitary	Influence students	Exhaustion	Higher education
Catherine	Medicine	Informal teaching	Make a difference	Disillusion	Medicine
Erika	English	Less solitary	Social justice	Stress	Flexibility and support
Jennifer	Science	Informal teaching	More enjoyable	Disillusion	Broaden influence
Jeremy	Medicine	Informal teaching	Make a difference	Disillusion	Follow principles
Jordan	Medicine	Unclear career direction	Influence students	Workload and salary	Solitary career
Kaitlin	Community work	Experience	Make a difference	Stress	Community work
Kelsey	Anthropology	Informal teaching	Recognized career	Disillusion	Family needs
Lily	Educational policy	Experience	Temporary	Workload	Policy
Liana	Science	Informal teaching	Shorter preparation	Workload and disillusion	Broaden influence
Lora	Unclear	Unsure career direction	Social justice	Feels right	Improve the system
Mason	Physical therapy	Coaching	Influence students	Religious beliefs	Pastoral work
Miles	Medicine	Felt right	Gain educational skills	Contract issues	Broaden influence
Monica	Medicine	Pay off debt	Influence students	Exhaustion and salary	Medicine
Nina	Medicine	Informal teaching	Delay graduate school	Disillusion	Medicine
Patricia	Science policy	Informal teaching	Inform citizens	Stress	Flexibility and support
Sasha	Elementary education	More rigorous coursework	Influence students	Stress	Improve the system
Sidney	Law	Informal teaching	More enjoyable	Disillusion	Follow principles
Susan	Community work	Experience and personality	Make a difference	Contract issues	Community work

Additionally, ten of the twenty-five cited previous informal teaching experiences, such as tutoring, serving as a teaching assistant, or facilitating summer programs, as inspiration for their interest in working with young people, another common refrain in motivating teaching careers (e.g., Schutz, Crowder, and White 2001). For instance, Jennifer had partially completed a doctorate in chemistry when she was given her first job as a teaching assistant and became drawn to teaching. She explained, "I taught freshman chemistry and that's when I fell in love with teaching. I was like, this is so much better than working in a lab." Likewise, Amber said she had "absolutely no interest in getting certified to teach." However, after working at a summer program for at-risk youth, she "just fell in love with the experience of it" and decided to earn a master's degree in teaching.

Along with the prominent themes of making a difference and informal teaching experiences, an additional pattern also emerged for a substantial minority (nine of the twenty-five participants). These individuals were not only pulled to teaching, but they were also pushed away from their first-choice careers. They became dissatisfied or anxious about their choices for one reason or another and began to consider other options, including teaching. For instance, while working on her senior honors thesis, Erika noted: "Originally I was thinking I would get a Ph.D. and I decided against that. My thesis advisor just didn't make it seem appealing. She was like, it's going to be a lot of alone time. And I thought, maybe I'll do something else, maybe I'd like to be a teacher."

Liana was also considering a doctorate, but she was concerned about the extensive training required in the sciences, explaining, "It was a little bit that I was done with school but mostly I felt the prospect for getting a professorship was so low that I just didn't feel like putting myself through that and then not having a permanent job until I was 40." Others simply found they did not enjoy their original career choices as much as they expected. Sidney explained, "I started working at a law firm and that killed the dream," and Jordan noted, "I started volunteering at a hospital and I found out that I'm a little bit more squeamish than I realized, and I just started having all sorts of doubts associated with the whole medical school thing." These participants expressed a pull toward teaching as well as a push away from their original career paths.

Push and Pull in Leaving Teaching

While the life histories of these teacher leavers suggest a simultaneous push and pull in the selection of a teaching career, they also indicate a push and pull in their decisions to leave classroom teaching. Here again, teacher leavers did not offer one reason for leaving classroom teaching, but instead they cited a variety of factors both pushing them out of teaching and pulling them toward other careers. As might be expected, almost all the teacher leavers noted some level of dissatisfaction with their workplace context that pushed them out of teaching (DeAngelis and Presley 2011; Ladd 2011). Seventeen of the twenty-five teacher leavers mentioned disillusionment, exhaustion, stress, or excessive workload within their school context.

Lora explained that as a teacher, she felt complicit working in a system that was harming children, explaining, "I felt like I was in an oppressive environment and I was enabling this machine that I wanted to destroy. I didn't feel like I could kill it from within, I had to kill it from outside." She later returned to graduate school in education to work toward social justice goals. Erika expressed a similar sentiment: "I felt really traumatized by the experience. It was a very chaotic place, it was violent in some cases, and I felt like it was really like an abusive, toxic work environment." Jeremy also cited conflicts with colleagues who held more traditional philosophies of science teaching, noting, "I was getting pretty tired of having to fight constant battles just to maintain effective teaching." Another common refrain was ineffective administrators, mentioned by sixteen of the twenty-five teacher leavers, who believed their principals to be "vindictive" and "vengeful"' while they tried to "pit staff against each other."

Other teachers mentioned themes of exhaustion and overwork. Kaitlin felt her own brief teacher preparation did a disservice to herself and her students, noting, "I continued to really struggle to balance everything, to feel successful, to ensure that each student was challenged, to manage behavior. I didn't think [I was] benefiting the students to the degree [I] could." Kaitlin now works for city hall. Jordan, in her eighth year of teaching, also continued to feel overworked, noting, "I just felt like I was kind of drowning. I started to become disenchanted with everything—the system is so broken, and I'm overworked, and I'm underpaid." She later made a switch into computer science. And Lily simply noted, "This isn't fair. I shouldn't be doing all of this work. This isn't one person's job. This is three persons' job."

In addition to school-level frustrations, five of the twenty-five teacher leavers discussed contract or salary concerns that accelerated their departure from the classroom. Liana, who holds a physics degree, was placed in a second-grade science classroom. According to Liana, when her principal assigned her to teach "second grade, I said, okay, goodbye. Because she knew I didn't want second grade." Likewise, after over twenty years in the classroom, Miles started in a new district program, but his position was cut after only one year. After that experience, Miles explained, "I was so angry and so sad. I started to think that this was not a place for me." Susan's departure from teaching was also accelerated by anticipated district layoffs. She stated, "I got out one year ahead. There is about to be this wave of unemployed teachers. How am I going to differentiate myself from any of the rest of them? Most of them are young, over-educated white women."

Salary also came up as an influential concern for several teachers. Monica noted, "I work 100 hours a week, I repeat myself every day, and I can't afford to go on vacation. I'm turning 30 and I don't feel fulfilled." She is now in the process of applying to become a physician's assistant. Kaitlin raised concerns about her ability to buy a house on a teacher's salary "I was so stressed out, I was like how could I ever like buy a house in [this area] and continue at this job." And Andrew pursued school administration simply because it paid more to support his growing family.

In all, only four of the twenty-five teachers did not raise the issue of working conditions as part of their decisions to leave teaching. Only one teacher, Mason, who is now a pastor, explicitly mentioned that he was not dissatisfied with the field of education, noting, "None of the switches were because of ill-will. Yes there are concerns about the direction of education today, but those concerns never pushed me out." However, alongside these issues of working conditions pushing teachers out of the classroom, there was again a substantial minority of teachers who were also pulled toward other fields. Nine of the twenty-five teacher leavers explained that they were also pulled toward the salary, contribution, intellectual stimulation, or fit of other careers.

Susan, whose departure was accelerated by a coming wave of teacher layoffs, had already been making plans for some time to transition to the nonprofit sector. Her long-term goal was to serve a community in need, and she saw teaching as only one of many possible avenues for doing so, explaining: "My whole attitude is, what do I see that a community is looking for and can I plug in? Educational inequity seemed like an easy and a meaningful entry point. But there's also other social problems that are fascinating and really urgently need work." While teaching, Susan volunteered for a full year at an organization fighting homelessness, noting that she was "networking and positioning myself so that I could have a job."

Catherine offers another example of pull. She pursued premedical requirements during college and became interested in teaching after spending a summer in Africa writing curriculum for HIV/AIDS education. While Catherine dealt with frustrations with her school administration, she also was pulled back to her interest in medicine, stating, "I have this passion to care for the underserved. It may not be in the classroom, though." Here again, teacher leavers were both pushed from the classroom while also pulled toward other professional avenues.

Push and Pull around Teachers' Passions

A third theme of push and pull around teachers' passions emerged from the life histories of these twenty-five teacher leavers. On this theme of connectedness over time, Olsen (2008) writes, "I am guided by a view of teacher development as a continuum rather than discrete, linear parts" (23). We similarly found that teacher leavers expressed passions that guided them throughout their professional careers, pushing and pulling them into and out of classroom teaching at various points in time. These passions emerged as underlying currents that weaved throughout their professional pathways in various ways, and many felt that, by leaving classroom teaching, they were actually continuing along the same course. In this section, we highlight the experiences of two teacher leavers who reflected on the ways in which their career trajectories were pushed and pulled by guiding passions.

Kelsey

Pushing in with Passion. Kelsey began her life history explaining that, as a child, she loved dolphins and aspired to be a marine biologist. Interestingly, her father was a chemist and her mother an elementary schoolteacher, thus it seemed that science teaching would be a natural fit. But since a young age, Kelsey had her heart set on becoming a scientist rather than a teacher: "So my dad was a scientist and then he owned his own chemical company. So science was always kind of in the back of—not even in the back of my mind. That's what I knew I wanted to be, even though ironically enough, people told me my whole like because my mom is or was a teacher, and so people always were like, 'Oh, aren't you gonna just be such a great teacher.' And I was like, 'Oh, no. I don't want to be a teacher.'" Throughout her childhood, she was drawn to living things and loved animals. "That was just kind of my thing. I loved being around animals. I loved hanging out with animals." In college, she discovered the field of primatology, spent a summer doing primate research in Mexico, and intended to earn a doctorate in the field. During her senior year, however, she began to have doubts about her ability to live overseas conducting research for long periods of time.

Instead of going to graduate school, Kelsey decided to move with her future husband and work as a zookeeper at the local zoo, where she continued her interaction with animals. As she became disenchanted with her work at the zoo, coupled with the limited job opportunities and poor pay, Kelsey began seeking out other opportunities and started to consider teaching:

> And one thing that I did figure out when I was zoo-keeping, one of the things that all the zookeepers complained about was dealing with the public. That's one of the things that I really enjoyed. I had to do some of the daily talks to the public and I answered their questions and sometimes school groups would come through, and I really enjoyed that. And that whole education thing kind of started coming back to me. My love of science at that point was just like bursting. I want to teach and give other people this love of science. It was just coming out of me in every way at that point.

From this experience, she became inspired to share her love of science with others. Fueled by her passion for science, Kelsey applied to a master's program in education and started her journey into the teaching realm. She ended up earning teacher certifications in biology, chemistry, and general science.

Pulling out with Passion. Upon certification, Kelsey taught science for four years in the Midwest. While she expressed frustration with traditional colleagues, inconsistent administrators, and overzealous reform efforts, she generally enjoyed her time as a classroom teacher, particularly her relationships with the students. But, because of top-down pressures, the middle school was forced to focus all their energies on literacy development coupled with a scripted curriculum. Kelsey was quickly finding that her passion for science was stifled: "And it just kind of took away from actually teaching any science because we were constantly trying to teach the kids reading, and how to read, and it was weird and nobody liked it, and there were so many people who unhappy that it just made it kind of a really negative experience."

Because of contract issues, Kelsey ended up moving to a different school, but she calculated that in one school year, the teachers had to manage twelve different reform initiatives. "You're not gonna get results on any of those things [initiatives]. And so I was just really becoming disenchanted." Kelsey became disillusioned with the public education system overall, fearing that she was actually bringing harm to her students by participating in a broken system. She explained: "I just feel like the education system is so broken, the fact that it's rewarding all of these teachers who are doing rote memorization. And rewarding teachers who are getting through the material as quickly as possible and then students get to college and they have no idea what's going on. And universities are blaming the high schooler and the high school teachers are blaming the middle school teachers and the middle school teachers are blaming the elementary teachers. And so I just think that something needs to change."

Administrative and school initiatives fed into Kelsey's sense of disillusionment at the same time that she felt her passion was being undermined. She reasoned that this was the right time to get out of teaching. At the end of her fifth year, when Kelsey had two young children and her mother-in-law began having health problems, she and her husband made the decision to move back to his hometown to take over the family farm. Kelsey now stays home with her two children and raises 300 chickens as part of an egg business. Of this change in her career path, Kelsey notes, "I ended up coming back to taking care of animals."

Ayana

Pushing in with Passion. Ayana is a teacher leaver who began her life history discussing her passion for the arts. As a student, Ayana attended several high schools, switching so that she could participate more actively in the theater program. After studying theater in college and captaining the swim team, she was headed toward a performance career when she decided that she wanted to apply her passion for the arts toward a larger purpose. She explained, "I'm passionate about the arts, but there needs to be another connection for me. What is the purpose of doing this? I always wanted to work with at-risk populations within the context of art." Ayana took a job as a counselor at a "last chance" wilderness program for youth in trouble with the law. She explained, "I saw the connection. I could see the through line through everything that I've done."

After two years at the wilderness program, Ayana began to wonder if, as a classroom teacher, she could prevent some of the problems youth faced with juvenile delinquency rather than repair them after the fact. Ayana started to recognize that for the boys in the wilderness program, "The nail in the coffin for a lot of them happened at school. And if they had had teachers and people within the school system that handled them better than they might have learned—they just might have had different outcomes in their life." She realized that "If I become a teacher then I could stop people from getting in the system before they start." She applied to an alternative certification program and was placed in a biology classroom because of her experiences in nature.

Pulling out with Passion. Ayana taught science for three years in the South, where she explained, "I love teaching," but found the time commitment overwhelming, commenting, "If you're doing everything that you need to do as a teacher, you will never do anything else. You just cannot physically do it all. And I'm the type of person who like goes all in." What Ayana started to recognize about herself is that, "I love science, but it's not my passion," and her passion lay more within bringing the arts to children in need.

Ayana ultimately decided instead to take a position as an after-school program director in a college preparatory leadership program: "I decided to come here because I wanted to get back into the arts. I wanted to get back to that part of my life and share that with kids, because that's what I've always wanted to do. I believe in the power of the arts to help kids really become better thinkers." The program combined academics with health, arts, camping, travel, and community involvement. Ayana explained, "It kind of wrapped all of the things that are important to me in one program. And that felt like the through line of my life. All of it makes sense and preps me for what I do now."

Kelsey and Ayana exemplify the ways in which teachers' careers are pushed and pulled around their underlying passions. Kelsey maintained a passion for animals throughout various phases of her career. While teaching biology was one way to carry out that passion, she was ultimately pulled toward other venues for pursuing her love of animals. Likewise, Ayana discussed a "through line" in her life, referring to a sustained passion for the arts. Ayana carried out this passion in various professional roles, including (but not limited to) classroom teaching. Kelsey, Ayana, and other teacher leavers viewed the classroom as only one of many possible sites for pursuing their underlying passions.

Constructing a Teaching Career

We found that these teacher leavers used a complex interaction of pushes and pulls in the longitudinal construction of their lives and careers. As expected, there were structural factors pushing teachers from the classroom. However, teachers were also pulled toward more socially prestigious and attractive careers while negotiating coherence around their passions. Together, their experiences reinforce the Savickas (2012) and Savickas et al. (2009) perspectives that teachers actively construct their own life trajectories—not in response to singular factors but through a complex designing process that integrates pushes and pulls from within as well as outside of education.

These dynamics of push and pull suggest that not only intrinsic and extrinsic factors influence teachers' careers, but larger societal forces are also influential, as individuals consider teaching in the context of multiple career options. As Scott and colleagues (2001) suggest, it is not only the internal features of a teaching career, but that career in relation to larger societal trends, such as career status and professionalism, that influence teachers' career pathways. In their life histories, these teacher leavers emphasized how a push away from their original career interests sparked a pull toward teaching as well as how a push from a challenging school context was often paired with a pull toward a new professional direction. While some previous research has considered the financial or professional implications of choosing teaching in comparison with other fields (e.g., Johnson 2007; Murnane and Olsen 1990), our findings stress the need to situate teachers' personal and professional work lives among the larger trends affecting today's workforce (Dwyer and Wyn 2007).

Their experiences also underscore the fundamental necessity of increasing the attractiveness of a teaching career, to even more powerfully pull individuals toward teaching and keep them there. Our data show that only two of the twenty-five teacher leavers started out being interested in the field of education, suggesting that individuals must be somehow pulled toward teaching from other careers. Studies demonstrate that in countries where teaching commands higher status, it is easier to attract high-performing individuals into the profession (Barber and Mourshed 2007). Status may be a place to begin pulling individuals to teaching in the United States as well. While individuals negotiate their teaching careers in conjunction with other fields, certainly improving the working conditions in schools could pull them more forcefully toward the teaching profession for the benefit of schools, students, and the teachers themselves (Henry, Bastian, and Fortner 2011; Ingersoll and Merrill 2012; Carroll 2007).

Part II

Structural Factors in
Teacher Attrition

••••••••••••••••••••••

2

The Struggle Is Real

• • • • • • • • • • • • • • • • • • • •

Administrators, Teachers,
and the System

It would be hard to find someone who does not agree that the principal is the heartbeat and the foundation of a school. Past research has shown that principals, and the supports they offer, directly influence how teachers see their teaching practice, and more broadly, how they see themselves (Littrell et al. 1994). Johnson, Kraft, and Papay (2012) identify nine key elements leading to quality work environments for teachers, and one of these elements is the principal. Over the decades, new accountability policies for students as well as for teachers have put more influence on school leadership for the success, and even survival, of schools (Pierce 2014). In short, the "intrinsic empowerment of the workplace" in influencing the job satisfaction of teachers' lives is intimately connected (Davis and Wilson 2000) to the principal.

Therefore, it should not come as a surprise that 100 percent of the participating teacher leavers discussed their relationship with the school administration as one key variable influencing their decision to leave the classroom. Although administrators and teachers are often thought to work together as a team, we found fractures in these team structures to be a major catalyst for teachers' departures. Teachers reported that administrators adopted an "us versus them" mentality as well as "inner-circle" politics. It was often the administrators themselves, the systemic pressures on the administrators, or a combination of both that led teachers to decide to leave the profession.

School administrators in general, and administrators in urban districts in particular, have extremely challenging, demanding, and complicated jobs. This chapter acknowledges their efforts and contributions, while sharing the voices of the teachers who worked for them. In these life history interviews, we share stories of administrators who would stop at nothing to support their staff, as well as administrators who would undermine their efforts.

In this chapter, we present both approaches from the perspective of the teachers, first by sharing positive stories, followed by negative ones, and then we complete the chapter with positive, actionable goals. We do not intend to reinforce an "us versus them" mentality, but instead we aim to construct productive goals for strengthening the relationship between administrators and teachers for the benefit of all. This chapter begins by highlighting four types of support administrators provided to teachers. Then, we outline the teachers' perspectives on the challenges they experienced, as well as their underlying expectations for the administration. We follow the story of Erika, who was caught between the administration and union representation, as well as that of Nina, who experienced how administrative turnover and the system's influence impacted her career. This chapter demonstrates the importance of educational administrators in the career development of teachers. It also captures instances in which teachers turned to administrators for support, but found those supports limited or strained. The end of the chapter describes the implications emerging from the strained teacher-administrator relationships in particular, including the fundamental importance of establishing and maintaining trust among school personnel and fostering resilient school cultures.

Our intention in sharing the narratives is not to marginalize administration in schools. Rather, it is to show the critical importance of this relationship. The actions of some administrators influenced teachers' decisions to leave the field. But others provided ongoing support and fostered success—demonstrating how much the teachers valued this relationship.

Stories of Support and Success

When we conducted life histories with the teacher leavers, we heard of positive administrator relationships during their tenure as teachers. These were times when things were going smoothly in their careers, and the thought of leaving did not occur to the teacher leavers. The teacher leavers indicated there were four key approaches to urban school administration. (1) the radical administrator approach, (2) supporting creativity and freedom, (3) providing constructive feedback and communication, and (4) being a cheerleader. All four of these approaches led to positive administrator relationships. The

FIG. 2.1 The radical administrator approach

following snippets demonstrate these positive approaches to school administration.

The Radical Administrator Approach

In urban schools, there are many top-down reforms that often occur in a short amount of time. These external initiatives can be daunting for teachers, who are often still working to implement one reform when another arrives. We heard stories of radical administrators who pushed back against the external pressures from the school district. We call this the radical administrator approach: when a school leader absorbed the district's demands, only filtering through those that would have a positive impact for teachers. Figure 2.1 captures how administrators who followed this approach served as a buffer for teachers, protecting them against external forces and allowing them to focus on their classroom and students.

Sidney shared one example of the radical administrator approach. Sidney's principal, whom she still keeps in contact with and has a high regard for, was one of these radical administrators. At one point, the district handed down a scripted curriculum that teachers were required to read to the students, removing their professional autonomy and insight into the classroom. Sidney's principal, close to retirement and unconcerned with the consequences, told teachers they did not have to follow the scripted curriculum. She explained:

> My principal unofficially gave me the go ahead [to not follow a scripted curriculum]. If there were things that were from the district that we were supposed to be doing that made no sense, that weren't even aligned with what was on the [standardized exams]—I personally think they were trying to intentionally sink the scores that year so that the following year their new model would look more successful. My principal gave me the go ahead to not do what was mandated and to just teach. She knew I had this track record of being a great teacher. She wanted me to work with the kids. So that was awesome, just having someone who respected me and what I was doing.

Sidney's principal went out on a limb in her own career to do what she thought was best for her teachers and students. This ensured that the teachers felt less restricted and more respected in their efforts to support students academically.

Supporting Creativity and Freedom

Teacher leavers also talked about feeling a sense of freedom when their principals supported their creativity. Jeremy, for instance, shared a story of the dramatic shift from his first principal, who was unsupportive of new ideas, to the second principal, who saw the value in his approach and worked to replicate it across the school: "In my second year they hired a great guy who really wanted the best for kids as well. And so he and I got along very well, and still keep in contact now even though we both have moved on. So I think that was really helpful to me in shifting the culture of the school a little bit. Because when I first got there it was kind of like, 'Why are you doing these things different?' Later, it was, 'Why don't you do things like him?'"

After the administrative change, Jeremy felt more comfortable and freer to try new ideas in the classroom.

There is also the story of Miles, who worked with the same principal for twelve out of his twenty-three years of teaching, before the principal retired. His relationship with the principal was strong, as she was willing to listen to new ideas and offer support to carry them out. Miles explained:

> I've always worked with [Stephanie] and she was the kind of principal that if you were hard working and creative, you could do anything you wanted. And her goal was to help you with that, right. But if you were someone who came to her with an idea, she wouldn't take that idea on and do it for you, she would do the supporting. She'd say, "Let me know how I can help you with that." And so the people who came to her and she'd say, "Well, let me help you support you with that. Let me know what you need me to do."

The principal's supportiveness, in Miles case, led him and others to start an International Baccalaureate (IB) program in an urban school—in a place where only a few in urban schools exist in the United States. This came from the principal's willingness to listen and support her staff with initiatives important to them.

Providing Constructive Feedback and Communication

We found that teachers often yearned for constructive feedback. When it was not provided, it added to the frustrations and tensions between the administrator and teacher. On the other hand, when constructive feedback was offered willingly, it strengthened the trust and respect between the two parties.

Catherine loved her principal's feedback on her teaching evaluations. For example, the principal said, "'You know, this is really great, and I think this would push your teaching further,' and it was just very constructive and just lovely, but wasn't this big focus on that rating at the end of the year. It was a much more positive place to be." She compared this input to that of the vice principal, who instead told her, "Oh, this one paper was left on your bulletin board. You need to fix that."

The constructive feedback was particularly valued when it was reciprocal. Teachers appreciated when they could communicate feedback to the administrators directly, and when the feedback was valued and appreciated. Beatrice often completed her paperwork in a timely manner, and the administrators would often hold her up as a model in the school to other teachers. However, this made her feel as if she were being labeled as a token, and it made her feel quite uncomfortable. Beatrice then decided to provide this feedback directly to the administration, in this case, the department head and principal. She explained, "I was like let me just go talk to them and tell them I'm not comfortable with them doing that and there won't be any more issues, and that's what I did and it was fine." Beatrice felt comfortable sharing her constructive feedback with her principal and department head. This was a case where the feedback was valued and her request was honored.

Being a Cheerleader

There were times when the teachers doubted their ability to teach. Often, good administrators would be cheerleaders for the teachers, encouraging them during these low times. The reassurance would be a small, yet valued, piece of the administrator-teacher relationship. Kaitlin talked about how her principal was a champion for her. She explained: "I had a lot of self-doubt and felt like—and they [the principal and colleagues] all sort of patted me on the back a lot because I was just learning this totally new field. I was really only four years older than some of my students. I had a massive learning curve to catch up to both special ed and to teaching these multiple subjects." Just the small gestures, the encouragement, and the "pats on the back" from the principal and her colleagues were enough motivation to stay the course with teaching, for some time at least.

Vulnerable Novice Teachers and Administrative Pressures

The examples we have just shared illustrate the productive power of school principals in protecting, guiding, and supporting teachers in their work. However, at other times, the relationship between the teachers and their school administrators was more fraught and led to frustrations with the profession. This section shares some of those examples. For instance, many participants felt vulnerable with their principals, particularly when they were novice teachers and in unten-ured positions. They felt like they did not have a voice in the school, particu-larly when they had to say no.

Erika

Novice Taking on Veteran Roles. After completing her master's degree, Erika was delighted to land a job teaching at a public school within the same urban dis-trict. The district was restructuring to promote smaller-sized high schools, so this particular school was brand new and shared space with another established school. It happened to be located in a wealthy section, but it drew students from the lower-income regions of the city. This school was an all-girls school with a business theme.

From the time the school just opened, Erika, with all new teachers, ended up serving as the union representative during her first year of teaching, "which, looking back, was really a bad mistake. So I think that the principal, she sort of saw me as her potential lead teacher, eventually, and she wanted me in the union rep role because I think that she thought that I was going to be loyal to her." Encouraged by the principal, Erika took on this role, one often reserved for veteran, tenured teachers. For a first-year teacher, it is hard to refuse a posi-tion given by an administrator. Yet it was Erika's role as union representative that ultimately created tension with her administrator.

Whereas most union representatives may deal with only a handful of issues in a year, Erika unexpectedly had to take on more than she bargained for. She explained: "I guess I was thinking that I was gonna do the role—the actual role of being a union rep and there was numerous problems with the way that she had set up the school and violations of the contract and things like that. So I ended up needing to reach out to our district and try to resolve some of those. All the teachers were pretty disgruntled with the workload and the teaching load wasn't fair . . . there was all kinds of stuff that she did." For example, there was a schoolwide issue with teachers' hours of instruction being over the limit required by contract. The contract specified five 45-minute period classes with a required break after three periods back-to-back. But the reality was, "We had like 60-minute periods instead of 45-minute periods, so all the teachers were teaching like five classes but at 60 minutes, you know, that kind of thing." For example, "one teacher, in particular, the social studies teacher, she had all of the classes and she ended up teaching like two extra classes, you know, when you added up the minutes." Overscheduling was one of many other schoolwide grievances that Erika had to unexpectedly handle as the union representative.

Obviously, "the principal, of course, disagreed with [the grievances]. So there was like conflicts about that." The social studies teacher who advocated for her-self "ended up getting fired and she got her license revoked . . . [the principal] did not want her anymore and she found a way to get rid of her." Erika explained what occurred:

> [The social studies teacher] got fired on a technicality, having to do with her time. So that was a year where we had a mass transit strike and so the subways were shut down for several days and so the principal had actually asked people who had cars to go and like pick up other teachers so that we would be able to still make sure that we could keep the school open. And the social studies teacher, she ended up picking me up and we ended up sitting in traffic for a long time and she was a few hours late. And you know, we got a certain number of days that we can be absent. And she had taken, I guess, just too many days and the extra three hours like pushed her over the threshold and so she got fired. I mean that wasn't the real reason, but that's how [the principal] did it.

The principal's actions with the social studies teacher had an effect on Erika. Toward the end of the school year, Erika explained, "She had asked me to leave because of all the union stuff, and I felt like I was in a really bad position because I felt like if I had stayed she would have found a way to get rid of me." Erika knew from watching what had taken place with her colleagues that her principal would follow through on finding a way to get rid of Erika, so she decided to transfer to a different school within the same district.

From Bad to Worse. Erika transferred to this school, as a graduate-school friend had recommended it. This school was also new and in its second year when Erika started. Erika ended up "working there in the second and third year that it was open and that was a complete mess, it was a nightmare of a school." But Erika approached her position and role at the school differently than she had with her first experience. She stated, "So I knew better then to get involved in union matters at that point, so I just laid low and tried to just do my job but it was pretty miserable." Erika mentioned that the ills of the school again came down to the school principal. She elaborated: "I think it really boils down to the principal, she was just totally incompetent, and everything was designed to blame the teacher for everything, everything that went wrong. She had set it up so that the teacher would get blamed, and she did—I mean there was about 50 percent turnover every single year and she gave 30 percent of teachers unsatisfactories [on their evaluations] at the end of the year. You know, she was pretty useless too."

The situation with the principal was escalating with teachers, as well as with parents. Erika explained:

> When I was there people were like how is this woman still running this school, like everybody knew she was horrible. The parents were complaining. They

were going after the hierarchy at the Department of Ed, trying to get her out. Teachers were filing grievances and trying to go through the union to get her out. She was violating so many special ed laws and she was not providing services for ESL students and we had 30 kids in a class and no special ed teachers. We must have had 10 or 12 kids with special ed needs, not to mention the kids who are ESL and we had no support for that.

There were even violent incidents that occurred on school property, but "she brushed [it] under the rug. I mean stuff like that, and it was unbelievable, and we knew that she was doing funny stuff." The administrator's actions moved into illegal territory. During Erika's first year of teaching, she befriended a colleague that was responsible for entering grades for the school, as she knew the software system. In that situation, the colleague decided she had to leave because "the principal was asking her to change grades, basically, in the system. [The colleague] said she's [the administrator] not gonna protect me when this comes to light, like she's gonna throw me under the bus. She was in an impossible situation and if she refused the principal, the principal would have fired her." The colleague decided to put in the transfer. Interestingly, after Erika left the school, the principal was removed for grade tampering.

Erika felt validated that she was not alone when she came across the book *The Confessions of a Bad Teacher: The Shocking Truth from the Front Lines of American Public Education* by John Owens (2013). Owens was a publishing executive who decided to "give back" and ended up teaching at the very same school that Erika taught at, just a few years after she left. Owens' career as a teacher lasted only five months because the same principal gave him an "unsatisfactory" rating on his evaluation. Owens quit and chronicled his experiences, as well as his recommendations for public education, in his memoir. As Erika puts it, "looking back, just like it's ridiculous. I mean she—we were set up to fail from the beginning, you know. There's very few teachers that could have survived and flourished in that environment."

Erika went from a bad situation in her first school to a worse one at her second. She theorized, "I think if I hadn't been a union rep at the first place and I had just, you know, like, laid low and moved on at that [first] school, I think I would have done really—pretty well. It was only in retrospect that I realized how much worse it could get." Unfortunately, because of the stressors of her job, Erika began to develop health issues. She explained, "I'm not sure it was chicken and egg kind of thing, if I was struggling more in the school because of those health issues or the health issues were because I was struggling, you know, that kind of thing." Erika's health issues got so bad that "my doctor told me that I was not gonna be able to get better if I didn't quit this job. My husband was very supportive of me quitting, it was just too stressful. So I just quit without any other—I didn't have anything lined up, I just quit." Erika perservered until the end of the school year. Since it was her third year of teaching, she on the cusp of earning tenure. She simply explained, "I was about to get tenure and everybody thought I was crazy. I was like tenure means nothing when I don't want to teach anymore." The accumulated administrator pressures took their toll, and Erika walked out of the classroom door forever.

Administrator Turnover and the Systemic Influences

We often found that teachers were more inclined to cite the problem of constant turnover of specific administrators rather than the difficulties they experienced with specific administrators. As with the issue of teacher turnover, the revolving door of leadership strained the ability of teachers and administrators to develop mutually supportive and trusting relationships. But this constant turnover also exposed teachers to the whims of the district, leaving them without the protective barrier that so many desired. Nina's experience exemplifies this particular situation; for her it was not the tension that arose from dealing with one administrator, but rather the challenges of having several of them.

Nina

The Merry-Go-Round of Principals. Nina experienced principal turnover very quickly at her first school. The school was a charter school designed to teach students Arabic, but "A third of the kids were homeless, they came from homeless shelters and then very few of the kids were actually interested in learning Arabic. That was the whole point of the school. . . . There were probably like, ten kids who came straight from Yemen or Iraq who were spoke [Arabic], but then the rest were African American." Basically, the school population was not culturally connected to the Arabic language or culture, as the parents "were just not savvy enough to know how to apply to good schools." As in many urban school districts, it was hard for parents to understand how to go about advocating for their children and seeking out the best educational options. So most of the children at Nina's school were from the neighborhood and simply not interested in learning Arabic.

The first principal who opened the school, prior to Nina's employment, happened to be from the Arab world. Then the district "fired her because they thought she was associated with terrorists or something. And then she later won a racist suit against them because it was completely ludicrous." This situation started a whole series of principal turnovers that started before and continued during Nina's tenure, eventually leading to the school being shut down shortly after Nina's departure.

Nina said when she first started, "They had just gotten a new principal and then she left towards the end of the year. Like half-way, three-quarters through the year. She was just really incompetent." Sadly, Nina explained that she perceived this principal to be "frightened of children. She'd never come out of her office. All of her meetings would be about how to make a good bulletin board. It was a joke." At the end of the year, another principal came in, and, as Nina puts it, "I felt bad for the next guy to come in. This school was in shambles." After her second year of teaching there, and after coping with two more principals in the process (four within two years), Nina decided to seek out a more stable environment.

Systematic Pressures on Teacher-Administrator Relationships. Nina went to another charter school in the same city on the recommendation of a friend from graduate school. The school was more stable, and Nina's teaching schedule more manageable. Nina was also drawn to the school after meeting the principal. "She was really intelligent. She was very young. I think she used to be one of the youngest in the entire city. I think she was in her 30s or something when I came." Nina talked fondly about this administrator at the new school. The principal trusted Nina and her expertise in crafting an appropriate curriculum for her students. She explained: "The principal kind of let me do what I wanted. It was really nice. I got pigs to dissect and I got all this stuff. That was great. We did other experiments and stuff. I got chemicals and we used fire and all this stuff that I never had a chance to do. The kids were excited about learning; it was just a really great environment." Moreover, Nina appreciated how the principal enacted a teacher-centered approach to leadership. Nina shared, "She was focused more on instruction and how to get a good lesson across kind of thing as opposed to the appearance of having things look like people are learning, which I thought was great."

At this point in her career, Nina had been teaching middle-school general science. Moving into her sixth year of teaching, Nina taught a remedial science class, and she also suggested a physics class for the eleventh graders: "I'd always had really bad physics teachers growing up. I'd always had this feeling that I could do this better, so that's why I wanted to do it." Her principal was initially quite supportive of this idea, but her support wavered over time. However, this coincided with a time when top-down pressures from the district started to strain her relationship with her principal. Nina explained: "Something about it just still made me really angry. Even though I know the principal at my school was really an intelligent woman, she was still driven by these things that were coming from top down, like how schools were ranked or the grading of schools. So she would adjust her polices to kind of reflect that, which I didn't think necessarily was right."

Very slowly, Nina started to feel the shift in the principal's philosophy because of the outside pressures, which often centered on the pressure Nina faced with her remedial students. For instance, Nina's principal instructed her to focus her work on the students who were within reach of proficiency, rather than on those who were truly struggling: "I remember she really wanted to focus on students getting them to be from Level 3 to Level 4, so I would help teach these remedial classes after school and I remember her having me do just those Level 3 kids. But then you have all these Level 1 kids and they're like, well where's our class? And I'm like, I can't help. I'm only doing these kids. Those [Level 1] kids definitely needed a lot of help." The tensions between the administration and the system are what finally pushed Nina to leave teaching for medical school. She explained, "There was just really a combination of my experience first year and kind of being in a system where we weren't helping anyone. We were doing more harm than good. I mean I think at my second school I was definitely doing more good than harm but I don't know. I just kind of still felt dirty. . . . I didn't feel good about it."

In this case, Nina shows it is not just the individual interactions of teachers and administrators that are important, but that these interactions are shaped by the larger systemic context. When the ability of teachers and administrators to construct trust is challenged, reciprocal relationships can be strained by larger forces of accountability, limited resources, and turnover in the broader system. This can leave teachers feeling powerless in the face of the bureaucracy.

Recommendations

Although many teachers faced challenges working with school principals, Susan found a way to balance her relationship with her administrators by staying out of the way. She explained, "Usually administrators were just kind of like, wallpaper. I figured out I wanted to be in the sweet spot of don't be on anyone's shit list but don't be the shiny, shiny star either." Essentially, Susan found a way to work within the system by avoiding relationships with administrators in order to sustain herself in the school and the larger system. Susan recalled, "Once I got to the point where I could be a shiny, shiny star and started getting noticed by my principal, I was like, rut-ro. This is more work, more attention, more drama because it's like, when she has some idea that might or might not work, I don't actually want to get called for it first. Because I have my own agenda for what I'm running in my classroom."

Susan is referring to the old adage "no good deed goes unpunished." It is easy for administrators to want to focus on those teachers who will get the job done, but they also need to recognize that, with teachers' already burdensome job, this added attention could escalate teacher burnout. On the other hand, teachers should not feel as if they need to blend into the background. They should actively contribute to the school to the best of their ability.

Applying the Four Approaches

The teacher leavers' storied experiences provide a way to situate administrators in the eyes of their teachers through the four approaches: the radical administrator approach, supporting creativity and freedom, providing constructive feedback and communication, and being a cheerleader. Ultimately, these approaches highlight the importance for school administrators to foster a resilient school culture, and these four approaches will assist in constructing such a culture.

The approaches highlight the importance, in urban schools in particular, for school principals to work as mediators between teachers and the larger system. Principals do not have the final word within their school setting, but instead they are the intermediaries who translate larger policy and bring curricular initiatives into practice in their buildings. The inherent transitional nature of their role has caused problems, such as the one Nina shared. However, this role also provides principals with tremendous power to translate efforts in the best interests of their teachers and students. Principals who show a willingness to do what is best for students rather than thoughtlessly follow a prescription can earn the respect of teachers. However, teachers must also recognize the intermediary position of their school administrators—and the limitations of their leadership capacity.

Administrator Communication Network

For teacher educators, there are also many lessons to be learned from these storied experiences. First, it is important to counter the common "us verses them" mentality during the teacher-training process, and instead foster a positive, collaborative approach to working with administrators. A good way to do this is to include administrators in the courses. Specifically, teacher educators can set up what we call an *administrator communication network*. Often administrators are invited into teacher education classes only to recruit teachers or talk about career development (e.g., résumés, teacher interviews, etc.). This is a good start, but we would encourage teacher educators to push further. Invite administrators to come in and speak directly about other topics, such as new school reforms and their implementation into schools; how to effectively communicate with a principal; and what are principals' expectations when starting at a new school. The topics are endless, but setting up an administrator communication network can be beneficial to the preservice teachers, faculty, administrators, and university. This approach also models the important mentoring role that administrators can play in teachers' careers.

Building Communication Skills

Teacher educators can also work on directly building preservice teachers' communication skills. Relationship building is a two-way street, and it cannot be assumed that preservice teachers understand how to effectively communicate and display professional dispositions with administrators, particularly those who are just entering the workforce for the first time. In an age where face-to-face interaction is minimized by technology (e.g., email, texting/SMS, social media), this skill is becoming one that necessitates explicit instruction. Teaching communication skills also prepares preservice teachers to directly build these same communication skills with their future students. Encouraging preservice teachers to join professional organizations, such as the Association for Supervision and Curriculum Development (ASCD), may help them to gain a larger perspective on the role of administrators and the larger policy initiatives influencing their work.

Reflective Questions for Administrators

- What are the ways I can activate the radical administrator approach without jeopardizing my students, my teachers, and myself? What are the best ways to buffer teachers when needed?
- How can I most effectively communicate top-down initiatives into classroom practice? How do I make them seem sensible to teachers and students?
- Have I fostered respect and trust in my relationships with teachers? And do teachers have respectful and trusting relationships among themselves?

Reflective Questions for Teacher Educators

- Do I explicitly support preservice teachers in developing positive relationships with their administrators? Do I emphasize a mutually beneficial relationship or an "us versus them" mentality?
- How do I teach professional communication skills as part of my curriculum?
- What relationships have I made/can I make to develop an administrator communication network?

Suggested Readings for Administrators

Daresh, John C., and Jane Lynch. *Improve Learning by Building Community: A Principal's Guide to Action*. 2nd ed. Thousand Oaks, CA: Corwin Press, 2015.

> This book is specifically tailored to administrators, and it is focused on molding the school community (teachers and staff) for the betterment of students. It offers a shared

vision as the foundation of community building and provides specific strategies for developing, articulating, implementing, and monitoring that shared vision. It also considers the larger community by crafting mutually beneficial partnerships and sharing the collective school environment.

Suggested Readings for Teacher Educators

Cooper, Pamela J., and Cheri Simonds. *Communication for the Classroom Teacher*. 9th ed. New York: Pearson College Division, 2010.

This is a textbook that can easily be adopted into a teacher education course, such as a Foundations of Education course or a student-teaching seminar. The book is designed to provide specific strategies to incorporate communication skill building (e.g., listening, verbal, and nonverbal communication) into teacher educators' future/current classrooms, while also providing ideas for lesson plans on this topic. Multiple communication modalities are included. This is a great way for teacher educators to model the importance of professional communication for the preservice teachers and relate the information to their future pedagogical practice.

3

Wading through
the Waters

● ● ● ● ● ● ● ● ● ● ● ● ● ● ● ● ● ● ● ●

Exhaustion, Stress, and
Disillusionment with Teaching

It is no surprise that teaching is a stressful profession both emotionally and physically. The topic of stress has been so intimately and frequently discussed nationally (e.g., McCarthy et al. 2009; Stern and Brown 2016) and internationally (e.g., Song 2007; Yorimitsu, Houghton, and Taylor 2014) that it seems as if it is perceived to be an essential part of the profession. This stress can often lead to burnout. Burnout itself is often presented through three core dimensions: exhaustion, depersonalization/cynicism, and a lack of personal accomplishment (Maslach, Schaufeli, and Leiter 2001). Of these dimensions, emotional exhaustion figured most prominently in teacher leavers' decisions to leave. Eighty-eight percent of our participants admitted to being overly stressed and tired. The lack-of- personal-accomplishment dimension also played a central role, as 96 percent of our participants cited frustration with school systems leading to their disillusionment with teaching. Because of this exhaustion and disillusionment, many teacher leavers began seeking other career avenues where they could feel that their work mattered and made a difference.

While chapter 2 discussed the professional struggles of teacher leavers, this chapter looks at the emotional consequences of the decision to leave teaching. Professional decision-making is often seen as distinct from emotional experiences, but we found that the emotions of exhaustion, stress, and disillusionment were fundamental and often overpowering for teacher leavers. This chapter wades through the emotional component that contributed to our participants' decisions to leave, and concludes with concrete suggestions for supporting the emotional side of teachers' work.

Overworked, Exhausted, and the Never-Ending Grading

The participating former teachers described succumbing to exhaustion from the workload or the overbearing expectations of the job. Often the workload would creep into their personal lives. For example, Nina had friends in the business world who just did not understand why her workload as a teacher interfered with their weekend activities. "They really had no idea how much work went into it until they were trying to hang out on the weekend and I'm sitting there grading papers and like, I can't hang out. I have work to do," Nina recalled. Her story reflects the life history that Liana shared, when she first started dating her boyfriend (now husband), while working as a teacher: "Our dates would seriously be, I would go out to dinner, we'd come back, I would grade and he would type the grades into my grade book. I mean I couldn't even go to a movie. This would be a Saturday, I had no time ever. Fortunately, he works in the school so he understood, but I wanted to have a life." Jeremy got right to the point and explained, "The mounds of grading, I think, were wearing me down too."

Eventually the excessive amount of grading took its toll on the teachers. Lora discussed how the stress and emotional exhaustion would build up to the point of burnout: "Maybe you can handle it the first year is 'cause it takes so much energy. Like, okay, I got it, I got it. But then after a while, you just get burned out and you're just like okay, that's it, that's all I can handle. Put a fork [in me], I'm done." This scenario, where workload accumulates further and further, leading to exhaustion and ultimately burnout, was highlighted by Jordan's life history.

Jordan

Career Overview. Jordan was a classroom teacher for nine years. Although she did not set out to be a teacher, she ended up teaching science in the same city where she was born and raised. Jordan's career trajectory into science teaching was not a straightforward one. In high school, she explained, "I think I had a little bit of a fear of science." It was her AP Chemistry teacher who took time for her and strengthened her love for science. "I always had an interest in science," she remarked, "and I think the reason I was interested in it was because I was a little bit intimidated by it."

When Jordan entered college, her initial intent was to continue on to medical school after graduation. She majored in social work while also taking the prerequisite courses for premed majors. However, Jordan got a reality check on her career aspirations while volunteering at a local hospital: "I think what happened was I started volunteering at a hospital, and I found out that I'm a little bit more squeamish than I realized, and I just started having all sorts of doubts associated with the whole medical school thing." Graduation came and went, and Jordan was still indecisive about going to medical school. In the interim, her friend (who was a teacher) made the following suggestion: "'You could become a chemistry teacher. You have enough credits for that,' because there was at the time, they were doing all of these programs where you, even without a chemistry degree, you could fast track, 'cause there was such a shortage, into your license. So and I thought back on my experience in high school and having had so much apprehension about being in chemistry, and I thought if I was able to succeed in it, I could surely help other kids do the same thing, and so that's kind of how I ended up going into teaching."

Jordan decided to enter an alternative certification program that offered intensive training over the summer and a full-time teaching position in the fall. By the end of only one month of summer training, Jordan got a teaching job with the proviso that she continue in the program so that she could complete her certificate. She continued to take two to three classes per year while teaching in order to obtain her professional teaching license.

Jordan was teaching chemistry and conflict mediation at a performing arts–focused high school. A veteran science teacher was assigned as her mentor, and Jordan found that support to be helpful. Although the start of her teaching year was rocky, it ended up working out well: "So the first semester, there was like a lot of friction between me and the students, and I was getting angry and frustrated a lot. . . . I don't know what happened, but somehow at the end of that first semester, I just got it. And after that point, I was in love with it [teaching], and I had a great relationship with the kids." Jordan's relationship with her students grew stronger, the students' academic scores were improving dramatically, and Jordan decided, "I wanna keep doing this [teaching] for a long time."

Jordan was always a team player and willing to help out the school and its students; she took on new initiatives that were stimulating to her and supported the needs of the school community. When the physics teacher announced that she was leaving the school, the principal made plans to shut down the physics program—until Jordan volunteered to become the physics teacher. She ran the peer professional development program at her school. And she became the programmer at the school to help out the guidance office. In this role as a programmer, Jordan was in charge of making student and teacher schedules, and this experience provided, she said, "an inside look at the guidance department and how disorganized that was." She often ended up acting like a guidance counselor and assisting students with advising. Ultimately, "I think being the programmer gave me an inside look at how broken the school was in so many ways."

However, that "inside look" also raised some questions in Jordan's mind about how the school was being run. She was concerned about "money not being spent on the things that they're supposed to be spent on, just a lot of sort of like faking grades and kids being graduated that shouldn't have been, and kids being sort of confused in terms of like they'd go to the guidance counselor, and the guidance counselor had no idea what was going on or what class they were supposed to be in or how many credits they had." These questions led Jordan to begin questioning her career as a teacher: "Well, I had doubts probably around year five, and then stayed on for a couple more years, and then decided I needed to change schools. . . . I thought at that point that I might not want to continue with teaching because I had many frustrations at my first school. So I thought, 'Let me go to a school where I think it's going to be completely different, and if I still want to leave teaching after that, then it probably means that it's not for me.'"

Reasoning that another school environment might be better, Jordan moved to a different school within the same city. It also had a performing-arts focus, coupled with a reputation for high academic standards. For the students to be admitted, they had to demonstrate a certain academic achievement level along with great skill in their performance area (i.e., art, music, dance, etc.). However, rather than making the situation better, this change was the beginning of the end to Jordan's career in teaching.

Overworked and Underpaid. At the new school, Jordan's workload dramatically increased. She was given three subject areas to teach: chemistry, physics, and forensics. She had never taught forensics before and had no academic background in the area: "So that was a little bit intimidating because even though I was a seven-year teacher and I had written a ton of lessons, I was teaching to a completely different child, and I felt like I needed to rewrite all of my lessons from scratch, which I think is pretty reasonable. I don't think I was being overly ambitious or anything. I certainly didn't wanna rewrite everything from scratch, but I felt like it was necessary, and so when they gave me three preps, and two of them were test based, I knew I was gonna be really busy." It was as if Jordan was a first-year teacher all over again, prepping three classes with all new material. Moreover, Jordan had large class sizes and was asked to teach six courses, instead of the normal five-course workload: "When I got to the school, they asked me if I would teach an extra class, and normally, a teacher would teach five classes that are 45 minutes each. And they asked me if I would teach a sixth class for extra pay, of course, but they asked, but it was sort of one of those things where I felt like I should say yes, so I did. So I was teaching six classes, three different preps, and it equated to about 200 students." In addition, Jordan had to manage extra lab requirements from the city. She recalled, "When you teach a science class that's test based in [the city], you have to do a lab per week . . . the requirements of those kinds of courses, like the grading was just off the charts. It was sort of an impossible situation."

Jordan was struggling with extreme workload, high numbers of students, new preps; she tried but just could not keep up. She reached out to her administration for assistance: "I just felt like I was kind of drowning, and halfway through the year, I ended up asking my assistant principal, which I don't think I've ever done—I hadn't done in all my years of teaching—I said to her, 'I can't do this. I can't keep doing what I'm doing for another semester.' So she said, 'Okay, well, what if I give you—I take away the forensics class?' So I was down to just teaching chemistry and physics, so that was better, but it was still—the 200 students—it was a lot."

Even with this course reduction, Jordan still had other responsibilities tacked onto her job: "What ended up happening was whatever else needed to be done was added to my list of things to do. Those other teachers weren't necessarily doing a great job in the classroom. They didn't wanna spend the time to tutor after school, so I would get asked to tutor after school, so I would tutor after school, and then their students would come to me, and I would end up teaching their students." Jordan made it through the year. Even though she liked the new school and did not find much "political drama," she was still struggling with the extreme workload. "Nothing really much beyond the workload that was really troubling," she said. But the frustration was starting to build for Jordan: "It became frustrating, 'cause you feel like you're not getting monetarily compensated for this and like you're doing all this extra work, and it started to become a pretty big frustration."

It was after this first year of teaching at the new school (her eighth year of teaching overall) that Jordan knew she was exhausted and ready to quit the profession. As she explained, "I think as I started to sort of become disenchanted with everything. The system is so broken, and I'm overworked, and I'm underpaid." She did entertain the idea of going into a private school, but realized, "I didn't wanna experiment any further with it." It was during Jordan's ninth year of teaching that she started to make plans to transition out of teaching.

Seeking Solace in Isolation. As Jordan was planning her exit during her ninth year of teaching, she was struggling to figure out her new direction:

> I applied to some programs. I went back to medicine. I looked into what it would require for me to go into medicine. I think I applied to some post-bac programs. I thought maybe, well, not medicine. Then I looked into veterinary school or something like that, all these different kinds of—then I looked into

going into science for a PhD, and eventually, I ended up with computer science, but—which is—I guess it's related in the end. But, yeah, I ended up figuring that out at the last minute and getting into a program, so I was able to leave teaching during the summer of my ninth year.

The inspiration to go into computer science came in the same way as her initial inspiration to go into teaching—from an off-handed comment by a friend. This field was a thriving, high-demand industry with lots of opportunities for women. Jordan was able to receive a stipend while taking online computer programming courses for eight months.

Jordan realized that this transition was a perfect career fit, as it was based in science, but it also had isolation—which was something she was actively seeking: "[Computer programming] incorporates science, scientific thinking. It requires problem solving to do those math problems. It's like the same exact thing. But when you go into computer science, a lot of people were telling me, 'Well, you're gonna end up sitting at a desk and not talking to anybody all day.' And I thought, 'That sounds perfect after what I've been through.'" She reflects deeply about how her personality is more suited to isolated work:

> I'm also like a very introverted person, so like it was always a challenge for me to be up there in front of a roomful of kids, like commanding the room. It was sort of extra exhausting for me on top of that, so when I ended up with 34 kids in six classes, I think that was the last straw. So I was kind of looking forward to something that was a little bit more solitary, a little bit more like whatever I did, I was only in charge of me, and I wasn't gonna be held accountable for the test scores of all these people. It was just I think I just needed a relief from the intensity.

Furthermore, Jordan was also happy to be earning more income as a computer programmer. She explained that she "made more money just starting than I did my whole career as a teacher." Currently, Jordan sits happily at her isolated desk doing iOS development and writing applications for iPhones and iPads. But she provided an important reminder about overworked and emotionally exhausted teachers: "If I could've somehow not had been bombarded with maybe as much as I was, that I probably would've stayed in it longer."

Disillusioned

The teacher leavers' comments also reflected a second dimension of burnout: their disillusionment with the system. Often that disillusionment was due to school reforms, district policies, and administrative and governmental influences that were outside the confines of the classroom walls. After twenty-three years of teaching, Miles simply realized, "I'd also seen a window into the toxicity and the dysfunction of central office. I'd been in the system for almost 25 years, and it's the same crap that we've been dealing with year after year." Whereas Miles's disillusionment came from seeing the ills of the school district, Jeremy was frustrated with the need for constant student advocacy: "I think I was getting pretty tired of having to fight constant battles just to maintain effective teaching. So, as a exemplar of this, my fifth year I got a lot of my colleagues to say maybe multiple-choice tests aren't the best way to always assess students . . . This step took five years."

For Anita, it was the overarching political reforms that disillusioned her and caused frustration with the profession. After seventeen years of teaching, Anita was being confronted with the nationwide reform of No Child Left Behind (NCLB): "And then NCLB came along and really, really started banging down my door. So in the 7 years I taught there we went from testing 8 days a year to 28 days a year so I lost 6 weeks of instructional time to standardized testing." Anita, a nationally board certified science teacher, found herself responsible for teaching a reading class instead because a new reform effort required every teacher in the school to teach a reading class to their homeroom students. This whole process encouraged Anita to leave the job after almost two decades of teaching. She explained, "It was insane and I just felt like I was abusing students because I was testing them so much and these are 13-year-olds and they've been through all these tests and they were sick of it and I was sick of it. I didn't want to do it [teach] anymore."

Nina, whose experiences were similar to Anita's, also felt the system was broken. She said it was like "being in a system where we weren't helping anyone. We were doing more harm than good." This sense of disillusionment was best captured in Sidney's storied experience.

Sidney

Career Overview. After graduating from high school at the age of sixteen, Sidney remarked that she "really lacked focus and direction." She went to a university near her home, and she was indecisive as to her career path. Sidney explained, "I had so many majors. I was doing journalism. I was just kind of taking classes. . . . I technically had a major, I don't remember what it was at this point."

After visiting a friend at her university out of state, Sidney decided to transfer to the same school: "I transferred into [the university] as a broadcasting/telecommunications mass media major. I kind of flipped around between the different majors in that department, which has journalism, public relations. Then I started taking history classes and I really liked it. I wanted to go to law school. History is a good pre-law major so I stuck with history." Sidney successfully graduated with her bachelor's degree in history and immediately started working at a law firm. She despised the work at the law firm, which put an end to her dream of becoming a lawyer, but the experience highlighted the possibility of teaching: "I started working at a law firm and that killed the dreams. Also, really, I didn't want to do three years of law school. At the time that seemed like such an undertaking. And also I was thinking about doing law school but more with a child advocacy focus. I thought, maybe go into teaching."

Interestingly, the idea of becoming a teacher was not a new one. As a child, Sidney did not consider it as a career because her mother was a teacher, and Sidney defied the idea of becoming one herself: "I think that I was resistant to going into teaching as I was growing up because my mom was a teacher. I didn't wanna be compared, like, 'Oh, you're following in your mother's footsteps.' So I think I was always kind of drawn to teaching. When I was doing my undergrad at [my university] I volunteered with the GEAR UP Program. I was always drawn to working with young people but I think there was a little resistance from not wanting to be like my mom." Sidney decided to embrace the teaching profession, and she pursued her master's degree in teaching. This decision required a high level of commitment on Sidney's part, as she also needed to take a number of general education requirements that were missing from her bachelor's degree. Moreover, she switched to another office job that had a more convenient location to her graduate school. She worked during the day and went to graduate school part-time at night. It took her three years to complete her degree.

When it came time to student teach, Sidney had to quit her job. She ended up being placed in one of the top schools in the urban district. This was coupled with a wonderful cooperating teacher: "My cooperating teacher, she was actually finishing her PhD at [a university] in Ed Psych but she is committed to being a classroom teacher for life. She's a model teacher that they would always send struggling teachers to observe her. That was a really rewarding experience." Right before Sidney's graduation in June, by which time she had completed three teaching certifications (elementary, English/literacy, and social studies), she was able to obtain a job in the same school district. She became a seventh- and eighth-grade literacy and social studies teacher. The school was a feeder school from the local housing project, and it was high performing, consistently achieving their school benchmarks (Annual Yearly Progress—AYP) every year. Because it was a small school, the teachers had to take on extra responsibilities: "It was a lot of work because it's a small school. It's only one class per grade. It was pretty much like having a self-contained class because you never repeated a lesson. So it was a lot of planning, especially with coming up with the guided reading for two different grades."

Aside from the constant lesson preparations as a new teacher, her position as a literacy teacher provided extra stressors, as it was a subject area in which students received the state standardized test. She recalled, "I'm just getting acclimated to the pressure of the testing as a literacy teacher. There was some chaos in the school the year before I came in. There was a new principal who came in the year before I came in and that's who hired me, but he just drove out a lot of the old staff members. So the prior year's scores, I think, reflected the teacher morale in that they were low. There was a lot of pressure to get the scores up." Although Sidney had all these pressures, she had a supportive administration to help her through the process:

> There was an amazing curriculum and instruction director that was assigned just to our region. She would come in and work with me on things, so just having that level of support. I also had a school-based leader who was phenomenal. I look at people who are starting teaching now and I think no matter how well-prepared you are, you need people that are accessible in order to help you, in the moment, when you need that help. I think I was very fortunate that I came in—if I'd come in a year later I wouldn't have had those resources.

The curriculum and instruction director along with the school-based leader were supportive, but Sidney had more challenging interactions with the school principal. She stated, "I think that as a new principal he came in with something to prove and really rubbed people the wrong way. The way I've pieced it together, looking back, is I think he was trying to create divisions among the staff to prevent that from happening again. He would kind of play staff members off one another." Luckily, the principal left after the first year, and Sidney's second year in the school was phenomenal for two reasons: she looped with her seventh-grade students, and the new principal was far more supportive: "That was interesting because the seventh graders, I had them again as eighth graders. I had them for two years so that was awesome. My second year was a lot more rewarding just because the difficult principal left and a new principal came in and she was very laid back and just allowed teachers to have autonomy."

Following in the footsteps of her cooperating teacher, Sidney decided to earn her PhD part-time while teaching. She loved her experience at her school, but she also felt led to teach in a more challenging environment:

> The first school, it's very high poverty but it's stable. It's been a consistent school for decades. Then my second year I had really great year but I just really felt this calling to work in a more high-poverty, low-performing school. Because also at that point I had had such success with getting my students' test scores up and things like that. Also, I was starting my PhD program. I also wanted to get away from having so many preps so if I'd went to a traditional middle school, then I could teach three sections of seventh grade and only have to plan for one class.

School Reform and Bureaucratic Structure Overload. Sidney moved to a new school that was lower performing. She was surprised to find it was very stable, but she credited that to the principals' dedication to her staff and students. This same year, the large, urban school district received a new superintendent who was introducing "Rebirth Schools Initiative." This initiative was focused on improving underachieving schools through a "turnaround school" model. This initiative provided, as cited by the district, "the most drastic interventions," re-staffing the whole school with a new principal, teachers, and school personnel. If after a certain time the schools were still not performing well, they would be closed in the district, and then they were often transformed into a charter school. Despite the turmoil brought on by this reform initiative, Sidney's teaching colleagues wanted to stay on to demonstrate commitment to their students. She recalled, "I actually wrote the proposal to get the school kept as a [Rebirth] School instead of converted to a charter and got people on board signing—like teachers signing, saying, 'We wanna stay on and do this.' There was a core group of us that wanted to stay and transform the school." Under this school reform initiative, teachers have the option to reapply for their jobs, but the school district did not communicate this effectively to the school: "But I didn't stay because the school district didn't communicate anything to us as far as what the process was going to be about reapplying for our jobs. They also would not tell us who the principal was going to be. We wanted to stay with the [current] principal. Then it became clear that they weren't going to have her stay. They told us that we could go ahead and apply for other jobs but that if we site-selected to another position and then we ended up wanting to stay, we could rescind our agreements."

Although she was reluctant to change schools, Sidney was officially transferred into a magnet high school within the same district. She made this decision as an act of self-care in the face of this overwhelming and unrelenting school reform: "I just had to do what was best for me at the time. Just not knowing even what the school day was going to look like for the [Rebirth] School, and things like having the staff have uniforms to wear. I felt that that was insulting. Also during that year they switched over to all of these scripted curricula. All these scripted curriculum where you're reading and the kids are, it's like call and response so it wasn't really teaching. That was also an issue for me, is not being able to teach." This decision did not come without regret. Sidney explained, "My first year at the high school I really felt like I abandoned the kids at [the middle school] in a big way. I had a lot of regret and kind of beat myself up about that, I think, too much."

Students had to demonstrate a certain level of academic achievement to be admitted into Sidney's new magnet school, even though it was a public school. But despite their high test scores, Sidney still found that many of her students were academically unprepared: "Most of what got them into the school was their test scores. We know that the test scores are not valid based on all of the cheating and things in the school district. So I think that there were a lot of kids who had high test scores and got into the school who were not as academically prepared as the administration believed them to be." This differential provided a large variance in students' abilities within Sidney's class: "[It] was definitely a challenge. Looking in my classroom and having kids who are very advanced, as far as their academic readiness, but then also having kids who—like there were certain schools who, 'Wow, why do all the kids from that school have advanced [standardized test scores], but they're not reading on level?' You'd start to see these trends. That was challenging. Just having the expectation of teaching at such a high level but then the students not necessarily being at that level. That was a challenge."

Unlike her last school where there was a large community of teachers working together, at the new school Sidney felt isolated, lacked community, received little support from the principal, and observed unethical practices, such as pressure to change students' grades. She said, "It was very isolating. Then I think the way the principal tried to create separation between people definitely played a role." Furthermore, Sidney was at a school that represented an antithesis to her "calling" to work with high-needs schools all because of the bureaucratic ills of the school district. Sidney taught at this high school for three years, but eventually, "I was just at this point where my heart wasn't really in it, working with the more middle-class kids. I felt like they weren't as appreciative of teachers. I didn't feel as respected as I did in other school environments."

Sidney started to become so disillusioned with the school as well as the whole teaching profession: "For me [the challenge] was just working within a bureaucratic structure." It then came to a point where Sidney's teaching lacked its previous passion: "I wasn't passionate about it my last year. I kind of felt like I was just clocking in. I came to this point where I was either going to quit my PhD program and try to site-select to [a high-needs school] or I was going to resign from teaching and go the academic route. That was a really difficult decision." Sidney was very careful when she made this decision to leave teaching. She was so emotional about deciding what to do that she went to see a therapist every week for a month while making the decision. She also sought counsel from her peers. But then "I just got to the point where I was like, 'I have to take this leap of faith and do it and make a transition.' I just wasn't happy. Looking back now, over a year later, I kinda wish that I had resigned a year earlier. Just because that last year I really was just kinda clockin' in."

After spending years in a broken bureaucratic structure leading to disillusionment, Sidney walked away from her six-year teaching career and decided to move into higher education full time. "But," she exclaimed, "I feel like I have kind of like this unfinished work, like unfinished business to do with urban schools in [the district]. So I'm trying to think more of my research as filling that void. I think it goes back to [the middle school] and feeling almost forced out from there."

Recommendations

Managing Stress

Stress, burnout, and disillusionment can often be contagious. For administrators, it is important to provide outlets for teachers to preemptively manage their stress. There are various resources, and even schoolwide initiatives, that administrators can employ for their teachers and staff. An example of this is partnering with the Inner Resilience Program (http://www.innerresilience-tidescenter .org). The organization was established to provide social and emotional supports for teachers. The program offers various activities and services, including the Nurturing the Inner Life Series, a monthly afterschool group meeting at a school in which "through interactive exercises, individual reflection, and small group discussion, educators explore the skills needed to stay centered in times of stress." The organization also offers day-long and weekend residential retreats for teachers, where educators learn "strategies for staying calm, strong, and creative amidst the stresses of work and life. Participants take home practical tools for keeping alive a sense of purpose in their work."

For teacher educators, it is important to help guide preservice teachers on how to have healthy stress-relieving habits early in their career path. For example, Lynnette does the following activity with her student teachers to establish accountability partners before going into their student-teaching classroom. Each preservice teacher gets two index cards. On the index cards, they are instructed to write one activity that is going to "fill their spirit" during a week. They are asked to be specific about the details. The only stipulation is that schoolwork (i.e., grading papers, etc.) should not be conducted during this activity. Various examples of what preservice teachers have written on their index cards in the past include:

- Go for a long run on Sundays
- Watch my favorite television show for one hour on Wednesdays
- Meet at a café with friends on Friday evenings
- Spend one hour knitting on Mondays and Thursdays

One index card is given to another preservice teacher in the capstone class who is designed to be the preservice teacher's accountability partner. The accountability partner texts/SMS messages the partner to see if he or she has completed the activity every week. The other index card is given to the professor. Midway into student teaching when the workload becomes heavy and the student teachers' emotions are heightened, the professor brings the index cards to the capstone class to check in and see how the preservice teachers are doing with their self-care process and progress. This is the time in the semester when student teachers often compromise their self-care, so this activity is a great way to bring them back to the importance of their own emotional and physical health.

Reducing Workload

In addition to supporting teachers as they cope with the stressors that already exist at their jobs, a second approach is to provide a more sustainable workload for teachers. Many successful countries around the world actually require fewer hours of contact time with students each day; instead, they provide teachers with additional independent planning time, collaborative team meeting time, and time simply for thought and reflection on their work (Sahlberg 2010). Schools in the United States might consider restructuring the way teacher work is organized each workday in order to provide some of these benefits to their teachers as well. This effort would further support student achievement and reduce stress and exhaustion for the teachers themselves.

Although at first it seems that such a restructuring might require a substantial investment in funds, some simple reorganization of the teacher workload may accomplish this same goal. Teaching assignments are often awarded based on seniority, with the more experienced teachers receiving the most desirable courses and highest-achieving students. However, we might consider reversing this approach to acknowledge that newer teachers are working overtime to prepare new courses and develop their own pedagogical strategies. Perhaps a phased-in approach, in which novice teachers receive a reduced and well-supported teaching load, might eliminate some of the stress that comes at the beginning of the teachers' careers. School administrators might take on some of their teaching tasks to stay current with the work of teaching, modeling a successful approach that has been adopted in other nations (Sahlberg 2010). This approach would create a more equitable system for all, reducing the stress, exhaustion, and ultimate burnout that often come with an overly demanding workload.

Reflective Questions for Administrators
- Are there systems in place to provide stress relief for the teachers and staff? (e.g., mentors, mindfulness practices, etc.)
- Is the workload equitable for all teachers? Are new teachers provided with additional release time to prepare new courses?
- Are administrators and veteran teachers carrying their share of the load?

Reflective Questions for Teacher Educators

- What types of emotional accountability measures have I established for the student teachers?
- Are there stress-relief activities I can incorporate into my lesson plans as a model for teacher candidates?
- Have I prepared my future educators with the right questions to ask during job interviews? Will they be able to recognize a school with an unreasonable workload? Do they know how to advocate for themselves to get the time for preparation and reflection that they deserve?

Suggested Readings for Administration

Herman, Keith C., and Wendy M. Reinke. *Stress Management for Teachers: A Proactive Guide.* New York: Guilford Publications, 2014.

This book presents specific strategies for developing greater awareness of stress and teacher wellness, presented through teachers' storied experiences. It is appropriate for administrators as it is specifically designed for teacher workshops with accompanying downloadable materials to share with the faculty. There are individual and group exercises in each chapter, which fits well with professional development for teachers around coping with stress. Further, there is a specific chapter for school administrators and other school professionals on how to assess perceptions and tips on how to support teacher wellness. The book goes further to apply the Teacher Coach Model (TCM) framework to the stresses administrators encounter on the job, and it promotes the establishment of TCM study groups for continued encouragement.

Rankin, Jenny Grant. *First Aid for Teacher Burnout: How You Can Find Peace and Success.* New York: Routledge, 2016.

This book is written for both current and preservice teachers, focusing on how to heal the wounds of burnout or prevent burnout in the first place. The book covers a variety of topics from gaining the right mindset to how to dialogue with administrators. There are various assessments, electronic resources, and reflective exercises that teachers and preservice teachers can actively work on for building supports and strategies to prevent and deal with burnout. This is a great resource for administrators to share with their teachers. It also explains how to avoid or recognize burnout in the teaching staff and how to deal with it in a healthy manner in order to retain great teachers.

Sahlberg, P. *Finnish Lessons: What Can the World Learn from Educational Change in Finland?* New York: Teachers College Press, 2010.

Finland has one of the world's most successful school systems. This book emphasizes throughout that the secret to Finland's success is in placing a top priority on high-quality teachers. Sahlberg highlights features of the Finnish educational system, such as admission to teacher education, the teacher preparation process, the work of teachers as researchers, and the time devoted to reflection and pedagogical development. By gaining a deeper understanding of the central role of teachers in the Finnish educational system, readers also come to understand what Sahlberg terms the "Finnish paradox"—that less is actually more. This book provides an excellent perspective on the U.S. educational system and offers concrete strategies that can be applied for the benefit of students and teachers.

Suggested Readings for Teacher Educators

Hanh, Thich Nhat, and Katherine Weare. *Happy Teachers Change the World: A Guide for Cultivating Mindfulness in Education*. New York: Penguin Random House. 2017.

The lead author is the foremost authority on mindfulness, and this book is specifically tailored for teachers within K–12 schools and universities. The book provides detailed steps on how to be a mindful teacher by dealing with everyday activities (e.g., breathing, sitting, eating, etc.) to cultivating the practice of mindfulness in the classroom, school, and university contexts. The book includes storied experiences from teachers, practitioners, and other school personnel (e.g., school counselors, occupational therapists, etc.) concerning their own mindfulness practices. This is a great book for teacher educators to incorporate into their required reading. It also provides techniques that teacher educators can practice in class with their preservice teachers as a model for their future work.

Hemms, Kerry, and Graham White. *Teacher's Field Guide: 7 Truths about Teaching to Help You Start off Strong, Avoid Burnout, and Stay in Love with Teaching*. New York: Morgan James Publishing. 2017.

The lead author of this book has been an award-winning master teacher for over twenty years. It is presented through the voice of a veteran teacher passing down advice and knowledge to new and novice teachers. The book provides tools, tips, and strategies for dealing with internal stressors (e.g., mindset) to external stressors (e.g., workload, classroom management). Each chapter opens with a guiding question to think about that helps frame an application to the new teachers' lives. The book is very practical in nature, and it is a great resource to use with student teachers during their practicum and internship experiences.

4

Where Has All the Job Security Gone?

∙∙∙∙∙∙∙∙∙∙∙∙∙∙∙∙∙∙∙∙∙∙

Teaching is commonly known to be a stable career choice for college graduates. Lortie's (1975) early work on the socialization of teachers showed that many future educators, and male educators in particular, chose the profession because of its job security. Although teachers report prioritizing intrinsic rewards over extrinsic benefits (e.g., Schutz, Crowder, and White 2001; Nieto 2005), teaching nevertheless holds a reputation in the popular media and culture as a stable career (Hu 2010). This was not always the case, however, as historically teachers moved around quite a bit among locations and vocations, and in the last century teachers' careers have become relatively long-lasting and stable (Rury 1989).

Goldring, Taie, and Riddles' (2014) research into the satisfaction of teachers who have left the classroom demonstrates higher levels of satisfaction outside of education, with the exception of job security. Outside the classroom, teacher leavers were more satisfied with their salaries, work/life balance, opportunities to make a difference, sense of personal accomplishment, professional prestige, and thirteen other areas defined in this study. They only reported decreased satisfaction in benefits and job security.

Some of the distinctive features of the teaching profession that lead to stability are unions and the tenure system in public schools. Initially put into place in the early 1900s, teachers' unions and teacher tenure protected educators from a system in which they were often overworked and underpaid (Tyack 1974). Although today these features play a less vital role in the teaching profession

(Farkas, Johnson, and Duffett 2003), and some current educators hold more mixed views about their benefits (Johnson and Duffett 2003), many teachers do report positive views of the protections and stability offered by teachers' unions and teacher tenure (Qazilbash 2007) in protecting educators against unfair treatment.

However, these traditional features of stability in the teaching profession have been undermined for several decades by the school choice and charter school movements, which by design do not offer teachers the security of tenure or unions. Instead, charter schools argue that by disempowering unions, prohibiting tenure, and weakening the connection to a central district office, they offer greater autonomy to teachers and principals at the school site (Whitman 2008). But these features are also directly correlated with higher levels of job insecurity for the teachers themselves (Malloy and Wohlstetter 2003).

We found that many of the participating teacher leavers reported great professional instability during their years in the classroom. While this typically was the case among beginning teachers, district and programmatic instability ultimately lead to the attrition of one long-standing educator, Miles, after twenty-three years of teaching. Some of the instability was due to outside forces, while at other points the participants chose to switch schools or teaching assignments as they sought out better working conditions. This chapter captures the experiences of those teachers who struggled with job insecurity during their time in the classroom. For them it was a struggle that ultimately drove them out of the profession.

Although the matters of job insecurity emerged again and again in our conversations with teacher leavers, it is nevertheless largely a hidden issue in the research literature. For the most part, common assumptions about teaching as a stable profession remain intact (Goldring, Taie, and Riddles 2014). A few scholars have highlighted the role of job security in shaping teachers' careers. Clandinin and colleagues (2015) describe the tensions around contracts as one of several factors leading to teacher attrition. Likewise, Johnson (2007) argues for attending to better matches in teaching assignments as key to supporting and sustaining teachers over the long term. However, many studies of teacher career development fail to recognize the role of job insecurity in eroding teachers' satisfaction with and commitment to the profession.

In her analysis of the 2007–2008 Beginning Teacher Longitudinal Study from the National Center for Educational Statistics, Kaiser (2011) highlights the role of contract issues in shaping the career paths of educators. Her research indicates that among those who changed schools, 21–27 percent did so because of a contract nonrenewal. Likewise, among those teachers who chose to leave, 31–35 percent did so because their contracts were not renewed. While this may initially appear to be due to poor teacher quality, in many districts contracts are not renewed because of seniority rules, budget cuts, or changes in student enrollment. Thus, Kaiser highlights an issue that is often unrecognized: that contract issues underlying job insecurity can lead to teacher departures.

However, the genuine job instability that exists for many teachers is critical because of its connection to Maslach et al.'s (2001) construction of burnout. Burnout includes three core dimensions: exhaustion, depersonalization/cynicism, and a lack of personal accomplishment, and as this chapter will show, all three are salient in this analysis. When teachers are not offered hiring matches that fit their skill set, when they are forced to develop new curricula again and again for new teaching assignments, or when a program they have invested in deeply is eliminated, they begin to burn out in their careers.

Overall Influence of Job Instability

Across all of the participating teacher leavers, 68 percent experienced at least one career move to a different school or assignment prior to leaving the profession. It is difficult to determine whether this figure is typical among the larger population. Kaiser's (2011) data indicate that approximately 10 percent of all beginning teachers move in any given year, thus the accumulation of these moves over time might reach 68 percent, given teachers' average duration of 7.08 years in the classroom. However, there were some teachers with an extraordinarily high number of moves; these teachers changed environments (e.g., school or assignment) up to five times during their years as classroom teachers. Although it is difficult to determine whether the participating teacher leavers' job moves reflect larger trends, their experiences certainly belie the image of teaching as a stable profession.

Although some of the moves were discretionary, in which teachers switched schools or assignments to seek out improved working conditions, the teacher leavers also experienced a number of obligatory school changes, assignment changes, and general contract tensions that were outside of their control. For instance, although Kelsey initially taught high school science, she switched after two years to a middle school classroom when her original position was eliminated due to budget cuts. In this move, Kelsey lost her mentor, her colleagues, and the deep investment she had made in developing a new environmental science curriculum for her students. Sasha faced a similar challenge when her English position was cut for budgetary reasons at the end of her first year in the classroom. Although she was kept on at the same school as a substitute, Sasha was frustrated with her new role, explaining, "They keep you on to sub classes, but you're getting paid suddenly like a sub and you're in this shitty position of literally just different classes every day. At one point I lost my shit when they had me subbing a gym class in an auditorium and they would not let the kids move."

Trained as a professional teacher, Sasha now found herself simply covering classes, at times in a manner that she did not make her feel comfortable.

Other teacher leavers experienced increased stress and exhaustion because of the instability of their jobs. As we discussed in chapter 3, after teaching chemistry and physics at one high school for seven years, Jordan decided to move to another high school with higher academic standards for students. At the new school, she was assigned to also take on a forensics course, content with which she had little familiarity. Her heavy load of two hundred students per semester, in combination with a new and unfamiliar course assignment, was instrumental in leading to Jordan's ultimate stress, exhaustion, and departure from the profession.

Further, Erika, although only in her first year as a teacher, was asked to serve as union representative for her school because all of the teachers were new and, in her perception, the principal found her to be "loyal." However, in this role Erika waded into the middle of contract negotiations with other teachers, an uncomfortable role for a colleague, and even had to reach out to the district directly regarding the principal's scheduling decisions with respect to frequency of breaks and field trips. Although Erika was not faced with contract issues that directly impacted her own position, the added stress of negotiating contracts and working conditions on behalf of her peers contributed to her frustrations with the profession.

In this chapter, we highlight in greater depth the experiences of three teachers, Miles, Liana, and Susan, as they navigated changes in their careers, and found that the insecurity itself was a fundamental frustration with the profession.

Liana

Career Overview. After majoring in physics at a prestigious liberal arts college, Liana initially intended to pursue a doctorate in the field and go into higher education. However, she began to have doubts about that career path, noting, "It was a little bit being done with school but mostly I felt that the prospect for getting a professorship was so low that I just didn't feel like putting myself through that and then not having a permanent job until I was 40."

With past experience as a tutor and a religious schoolteacher, Liana decided that she wanted to pursue teaching. Because she had no formal education background or certification, she applied for positions at private schools through a recruiter who came to campus. She was offered a job in a major Eastern city and accepted, entering a program that combined a reduced teaching load with teacher training.

When another teacher left midway through the year, Liana ended up teaching a full load. She particularly enjoyed the experiments in biology, but commented that in the first year "the learning curve was extremely steep."

After two years of teaching in two different private schools, Liana ran into some conflict with her department chair around contract issues. Although she "was more interested in the older kids" and "liked teaching the complex concepts," she was explicitly assigned to second grade. Liana recalled, "When it came to resign the contract, I kept asking her what my assignment was going to be the following year and she wouldn't tell me, she wouldn't tell me, she wouldn't tell me. So finally the day before the contracts were due, I said, I'm not going to sign this unless you tell me what my assignment is going to be. And she said, all second grade and I said, okay, goodbye. Because she knew I didn't want second grade."

After Liana left, she volunteered on a congressional campaign, which turned into a decade of working in politics.

Never the Same Thing Twice. Although Liana loved her work in politics, where she felt that she was really making a difference to her community, she missed the students. She explained, "I just missed the kids, I really like working with the kids. The problems I had were mostly with the adults. I really never had problems with my students; it was the adults that were exhausting." Liana returned to teaching, this time earning her master's degree in education while teaching at a public high school. At the new high school, Liana encountered many veteran teachers who did not have the time to guide her in the curriculum. She noted, "It was pretty exhausting, and I never felt like the teachers were particularly welcoming. There was a lot of things where I kept asking, how do you do this lab and the attitude was, you're wasting my time. Figure it out on your own. They seemed nice on a basic level but not really willing to spend their time to help you."

After Liana returned to teaching, she found herself with a new course preparation each year. In her first year, Liana was assigned to a new conceptual physics course for freshman; however, the district cut the program because of a mismatch with the county exams. In her second year, Liana's position was cut due to budget concerns, and she was rehired in a biology position. In her third year, she was fired and rehired again to teach a special biology course suited to the needs of English Language Learners. About this course Liana commented: "It was such an interesting bunch of kids. They were mostly older, they were mostly motivated to do well in school. It was an interesting challenge to be working with them and figuring out what they didn't know and what they needed to learn. It was a little frustrating that there was so much of a vocabulary barrier and there were these county tests that they had to take and I wouldn't realize the word "shrub" was going to be the problem." Although she enjoyed the challenge of this and other new courses, Liana felt that repeating them more than once would have given her the time to solidify her curriculum.

In her fourth year, when she was once again facing a fire and rehire situation due to budgetary issues, Liana decided to take a permanent middle school position. Unfortunately, the school had just adopted a new physical science course, and "I was again writing an entire curriculum from scratch." Liana found herself learning more new material and facing pressure from the administration to stick to the content, but she lacked the resources to teach the curriculum. This time it was the final straw. She noted, "So that was it, I said, I'm done. I'm done with teaching. I was just so tired, I couldn't do this anymore." Liana reflected on what ultimately drove her out of the classroom: "I just wish that teaching was structured differently. I wish it was more sustainable. But I think right now it's not sustainable and I wish it were. I'd still like to be teaching. The other thing is, as difficult as the kids are, the adults are way more difficult. That to me is a big part of the problem. If the school were more coordinated and we had more support and if they didn't keep changing the curriculum again three years later."

Liana ultimately left due to exhaustion, having taught four entirely new courses in four years. If she had been given the time and space to really develop expertise in one particular subject area and grade level, and support for that effort, she might have found the sustainability she desired.

Miles

Career Overview. Most of his life, Miles had his sights set on becoming a doctor. However, after graduating from college, when he needed to gain additional research experience to enhance his medical school application, he found the idea of being in a lab all day unappealing. So Miles decided instead to pursue a master's degree in teacher education, reasoning that "I would always be able to utilize the skills and understand the things that I had gained," once he became a physician. But his plans changed once Miles experienced the joy of teaching. He explained: "I student taught with the most amazing people and as far as cooperating teachers—it was actually a professional practice school—and I feel in love with it. Just felt like it was something I should do. And I said, 'Well, okay, so I can do that for ten years and then go back into medicine.' And that was my plan. And clearly that didn't happen. But, what did happen is I became really intensely interested in teaching and learning." Miles became what he considered not a content teacher, but a teacher of children, working in a magnet school as part of a mid-size urban district in the far northern region of the United States.

Considering Multiple Career Paths. About seven years into his career as a teacher, Miles came to a crossroads. He still held onto the idea of medical school in the back of his mind and took the Medical College Admissions Test (MCAT), on which he scored well enough to be admitted. However, at the same time he enrolled in an advanced institute for biology teachers, which really boosted his confidence. He noted, "In my undergraduate years, I had not felt science smart at all. I felt average at best. And going to [the institute] helped me to realize that I was actually quite intellectually gifted in the sciences." At the same time, his urban school was in the midst of starting an International Baccalaureate (IB) program, and he was involved in the curriculum development.

Faced with a decision and boosted by his success at the institute, as well as his excitement about the IB initiative, Miles chose to stay on as a teacher. He recalled, "I picked teaching. Which really was amazing in terms of the sense of self-efficacy that it gave me, right? Because I made it of my own volition. I made the choice. The choice was not made for me. And so I felt—was feeling really competent."

Growing New Programs. Miles thrived as an IB teacher in the content area and in a course called Theory of Knowledge, where he "wanted students to appreciate and come away with a love of learning and a sense of wonder about humans and how we can do all the things we can do. And how complex that is." He was also committed to students on a personal level, noting that he appreciated "the ability to make a difference in peoples' lives, in students' lives, and beyond meeting curricular goals. It was more important for me to help students see themselves as people who could learn, who were competent." During those same years, Miles also coached swimming, became a National Board Certified Teacher, and started to take courses toward his doctorate in science education.

At a gathering of colleagues from across his district, Miles engaged in a conversation about "being the change we wanted to see." Inspired by his exceptional experience as a student teacher in a professional practice school, Miles suggested starting one in the district. The school would use master teachers to mentor and nurture beginning educators in the profession. This idea resonated with the president of the teacher's association, who brought a proposal to the district. Soon Miles was on the planning committee for a new professional practice high school. He described the new school: "It was a program for over-aged, under-credit students. And so we took on 1,200 tenth, eleventh, and twelfth graders. And that was what we had dreamt about." Although not all aspects of the proposal were implemented as envisioned, Miles was hired when the school opened as the professional learning coordinator and the coordinator of university partnerships, and he was delighted to see his vision put into action.

Moving On. Unfortunately, as Miles put it, "the district lies," and after one year they decided to close the school and eliminate his position. Miles described his state of mind at that time:

And I was so angry, and so sad, at the district and I felt like this was an opportunity to do the reform that these central office people talk about all the time, especially the superintendent, and I was just so pissed. And I said, "This once in a lifetime golden opportunity, if I can't effect change here, it can't be done from inside." I'd also seen a window into the toxicity and the dysfunction of central office. You know, I'd been in the system for almost twenty-five years, and it's the same crap that we've been dealing with year after year, in spite of having radically different superintendents, radically different mindsets, radically different ideologies.

This experience led him to disillusionment not only with the central office in his district, but with the field overall. He noted, "I started to think that this was not a place for me."

After this disappointment, Miles decided not to return to classroom teaching. Instead, he accepted a position in higher education as a director of science education outreach while continuing to work on his dissertation for his doctorate degree. In this higher-education role, Miles felt that he could once again do meaningful work: "I feel pushed to reach my potential. And I don't mean externally pushed. I mean I felt like a gas in a room that just expands to fill, you know, how gases expand to fill their container. And I feel like I've had the opportunity to just sort of let my creativity and my abilities flow, and just haven't hit a wall yet, haven't hit an edge of the container."

Susan

Career Overview. Susan grew up with two parents who were involved in politics and went to college committed to civic engagement. As a political theory major in college, Susan paired her interest in policy with first-hand work in a nearby local, urban community. She explained, "I started doing more work that looked like service in solidarity with people who are marginalized." Susan spent her summers working with a nun in the local community, where she ran a program to care for child victims of violent trauma. She was also struck by the strength she found within a community that was perceived poorly by outsiders. Susan noted, "I found tremendous strength and tremendous resilience and power in moms, dad, grandparents, extended kinship networks. I was like this place has a really shitty reputation and it does not match at all to my experience." Susan noted that she also learned to "practice humility and acknowledge that when you're working in a community that's not your own you likely don't have nearly as much to offer as you might think."

Committed to her relationship with this community, Susan wanted to remain connected after graduation in order to "deepen my relationship and contribution to positivity" in this same community. However, she was not entirely sure what the contribution might look like. She reasoned: "I was just kind of looking, like okay, what can you do that's useful? You're not gonna run for city council when you're twenty-two. Be a foot soldier. Do something useful and learn from, continue to learn from the community that's around you. Teacher felt like a meaningful in." Susan reflected that among all the issues facing impoverished communities, education was one where she might be able to contribute: "My whole attitude is what do I see that a community is looking for and can I plug in? So I'm like, education inequity seemed like an easy entry point perhaps and a meaningful entry point."

Leaving the Community. Susan applied to Teach for America (TFA) and was accepted into the corps serving this same community. Although she was not completely bought into TFA's approach to urban schools, the program was the most viable option for her to receive her teaching certificate. However, after training, the city faced a budget crisis. Susan explained: "[The] city budget was completely frozen and taken over by the state so charter schools hired, but neighborhood public schools couldn't hire. I interviewed with a couple of charter schools. It was a disaster, because I knew, charter isn't the solution. School choice movement doesn't make sense to me as a sustainable choice for communities. Especially communities that are under-resourced. We're just creating more artificial cleavages within an already struggling system." Susan was unwilling to take a job in a charter school based on her principles, but facing a hiring freeze in neighborhood schools, Susan had to choose between forfeiting her position with TFA or moving to a nearby, much larger urban school district.

Although her heart was in the community where she had worked for many years, Susan reluctantly agreed to take a position in the larger district because she believed it would serve her and the community down the road. She recalled: "[It] is a much bigger community and not one that I had ever really had any interest in, but again it wasn't about building the TFA community, it was about building skills and having resources to go seek out and be of use to a different community that did have meaning to me." She ended up teaching middle school English for six years in this district. During that time, in response to "district rumblings about what it is gonna look like to force out teachers," Susan also earned certification in grades 7–12 English, 7–12 social studies, and 7–9 math and science. She noted, "I just sat for all the certs that I could kind of one by one."

Bringing Community Development into the Classroom. Susan noted that it took about four years until "I felt like my teaching practice was proficient to work in the environment that I was in." As a teacher, Susan held her students to high academic expectations, noting, "My goals for my students were to read on or above grade level," but she also had high personal expectations for them to "conduct themselves as people of good judgment and character and understand that their development was an intellectual development, but also a holistic development as a person." She held herself to the same standards, noting that she tried to "conduct myself in a way that was a role model for my students, so both to model ethical decision making and leadership. But also model a lifelong love of learning." She taught a summer program every year she was community organizing. After working with one seventh-grade group and learning that the plan was to combine this group with another group (for a class of forty-five students in the eighth grade), Susan volunteered to loop with the group, moving into the eighth grade with them and helping them prepare for the transition to high school.

Susan also saw herself as championing her students on a personal level, just as she had done in her community efforts during college. She commented, "I started looking more and more at my role as defending my students and families from bad policy and kind of acting as an umbrella." For instance, when a zero-tolerance policy for behavior was issued by the district, Susan decided, "I'm gonna use my judgment and see what works, what doesn't work for my students and I'm gonna apply the way I see fit."

Returning to the Community. After five years in the classroom, Susan began to construct what she termed her "long-term exit strategy." She saved money from her three jobs as teacher, summer instructor, and bartender because "I knew I was getting ready to make this next move." She planned to loop with her students and see them through to high school, then leave teaching for good. She noted, "I felt like I exited with as much dignity, and kind of like care and forward thinking as I probably could have done." The timing was also right for her departure because soon after she left, the district, as expected, closed a large number of schools due to decreased enrollment, including the school where she worked. Susan commented: "I got out one year ahead. I kinda saw that too. There is about to be this wave of unemployed teachers and how am I gonna differentiate myself from any of the rest of them, because most of them are young, overeducated white women. So, I'm like, I don't want to be in that mess. See you later." Although she had enough seniority to transfer to another building after the school closures, Susan was ready to leave teaching, return to the primary community where she wanted to work, and "make a contribution that seemed great."

Susan wanted to return to her initial career aspiration of "transforming communities in the way they want." She noted, "I want to be able to make a positive contribution to a community I care about. So let me do that in a way where, rather than reacting to public policy, I can be part of crafting it. That was my goal." Susan also explained that she had objectives, rather than specific positions in mind: "I worked with the attitude of think about the desired outcome and then back your way into a job. It was not about what's my next job with a capital J going to be. It's like what's the impact that I'm trying to have and what's the vocational path that leads me closest to that impact?" Although Susan left without another position secured, she had been volunteering for six months with a nonprofit organization working to end homelessness and break the cycle of poverty back in the community. She explained: "I didn't have the next thing lined up. I had been volunteering at [this non-profit] for a year, networking and positioning myself so that when I came back at the end of the summer, I could be a little bit of a known entity. And my goal was just get a job. Get your foot in the door doing anything and use that job, whatever it is, to springboard into something else that's actually what you want."

Susan took a $30,000 pay cut to leave teaching and enter the nonprofit sector on a temporary, grant-funded position in the community. Over time, she worked her way into a stable position at the same organization where she volunteered, although she was still earning $11,000 less than she earned in her teaching job. Here, she felt that she was addressing one of the most pressing community needs: "We could say flip the same thing on its side it would be like, what is the most pressing need? Even looking at basic, basic, basic needs. So more basic than education is, do you have a place to stay? Do you have shelter? That really intrigued me." Susan also felt she gained skills in the classroom that applied to her current work: "I really learned a lot in that space that's transferable to work that I do now around building politics and coalition building and facilitating group consensus. Some of those things I knew intuitively, but I got to practice them in really tough environments. I put on my teacher hat a lot with about 150 people who have been homeless at some point in their life and work in any of our businesses." Although Susan still struggles to maintain work/life balance, she said, "I really like my work as a connector."

Job Insecurity in a "Secure" Career

Liana, Miles, and Susan, among other participants, all experienced insecurity in what is generally considered to be a stable teaching profession. Liana was assigned to teach a different grade or subject during each of her six years in a classroom. Miles saw his "once in a lifetime" program for students eliminated by the district. And Susan was forced through a hiring freeze to leave the community where she was committed to making a positive contribution. Although these were not their only reasons for leaving the classroom, they contributed to an ongoing sense of professional insecurity in their lives as teachers. This sense may have been further heightened by their expectation, shaped through popular culture and attitudes, that teaching is a stable job.

However, their experiences were not unique. While a certain set of teachers, particularly those in consistently well-funded districts, with tenured positions, do find stability in their careers, many beginning teachers who do not work under those conditions actually experience quite a bit of instability. For instance, Ingersoll (1999) found that despite a common assumption that under-qualified teachers come from poor teacher training, it is actually mismatching in hiring that leads to poor qualifications for the grade level or subject area. His research shows that one-third of mathematics teachers, one-fourth of English teachers, one-fifth of science teachers, and one fifth of social studies teachers were teaching out of their certification areas; some had less than a minor in the field they were teaching.

Schools that tracked students by ability levels were less likely to have out-of-field teaching. With the recent trend toward inclusion classrooms (Oakes, Joseph, and Muir 2004), out-of-content teaching may be an unintended consequence.

Moreover, contractual instability may lead to reduced effectiveness. One study of effective teaching (OECD 2009) found that teachers with greater instability in their contractual status experienced higher levels of student discipline problems and lower levels of self-efficacy. While less effective teachers may have been able to obtain only temporary contracts, our research suggests that the reverse is also likely. An unstable or continually changing context could lead to greater student behavior issues and lower levels of confidence in the classroom due to the incessantly changing nature of the work. Clandinin et al. (2015) also suggest that transience itself may interfere with the identity-making process of a teacher, inhibiting the important sense of connection to schools, students, and the larger educational endeavor.

Finally, hiring assignments can also lead directly to higher rates of attrition in the field. Donaldson and Johnson (2010), in their analysis of TFA teachers in urban schools, found that teachers with more challenging teaching assignments, which they described as split grades, multiple subjects, or out-of-field classes, were more likely either to transfer into another teaching assignment or leave teaching altogether, showing a direct link between insecurity with respect to professional expertise and teachers' career trajectories.

Job Insecurity on the Road to Burnout

Not only does job insecurity lead to possible reduced effectiveness, but it is a clear road to teacher burnout. Maslach et al.'s (2001) dimensions of exhaustion, depersonalization/cynicism, and lack of personal accomplishment mirror the experiences of all three highlighted teacher leavers. Liana left the field exhausted and frustrated with the unsustainability of the work after developing curriculum after curriculum, never repeating the same material twice. Her experience reflects the exhaustion dimension of burnout. Likewise, Miles left the classroom following a sense of betrayal by the district when it eliminated his valued program. His experiences clearly illustrate the depersonalization/cynicism dimension of burnout. And Susan left in order to pursue her original goals and make an even greater positive contribution to the community. Susan's life history exemplifies the feeling of a lack of personal accomplishment inherent in burnout.

Their experiences also illustrate the importance of teacher autonomy and control, not only over the curriculum they teach, but also over their own career paths. Liana, Miles, and Susan all were compelled to respond to situations created by forces outside their control. Liana's professional options were continually shaped by contractual constraints, Miles witnessed the program in which he had invested so much cut after only one year, and Susan left the community she cared for due to larger political forces.

These experiences sit in direct conflict with what research indicates are key features of career satisfaction: autonomy and control. Darling-Hammond and Rothman (2011) have noted that teachers in the most effective school systems around the world are given a high level of autonomy over their careers, a feature valued by educators and administrators alike (Quartz et al. 2010; Firestone 2014). For instance, Miles commented on the self-efficacy he gained when he chose a teaching career for himself. The teacher leavers' lack of autonomy over their career pathways certainly contributed to career decisions leading to increased control.

Recommendations

Value Teachers' Specialized Expertise

The experiences of these teacher leavers suggest that they often felt like widgets, hired to do a specific job rather than developed as professionals. Perhaps because of the excessive workload on the part of the administrators or district-level personnel, often little thought was given to the teachers themselves when making hiring decisions or teaching assignments. These decisions seemed designed simply to put a teacher into an empty classroom, but the particulars of location, grade level, and content area actually mattered a great deal to the teachers themselves. They had invested years in training, curriculum development, and refinement of a particular set of expertise and often had an innate passion for their work. When removed from that area of expertise, the teachers not only lost something they cared about deeply but they were also compelled to develop a new specialized skill set.

Greater attention not only to the needs of the schools and students, but also the preferences, passions, and specialized skill sets of the teachers themselves can prevent multiple dimensions of teacher burnout. Rinke (2014) argues for listening to teachers and providing them with the space to shape their own career paths. From a practical standpoint, this can be accomplished through extensive interviewing, reflective essays, or collaborative dialogue with teachers. However, providing teachers with space to express their preferences and offering them genuine control over their own career paths is vital to developing them as people and as professionals.

Support Novices' Establishment in the Field

In many contexts, teaching can be hierarchical: educators with greater seniority get the security of tenure along with the most desirable grade levels, courses, and student assignments. While this provides some incentive for teachers to stay in the field long term to earn these benefits, it can also be a disincentive to novice educators struggling to establish themselves in the profession. As Liana noted, beginning teachers have a steep learning curve with respect to classroom management, pedagogy, and even content. To layer multiple curriculum changes or challenging or unwelcome teaching assignments on top of this task can be overwhelming for novice teachers and makes alternatives outside of education all the more attractive.

Rather than easing the workload for veteran teachers on the backs of novices, career ladders should be structured in such a way to protect beginning educators and allow them to focus on establishing themselves professionally. There are many pragmatic ways to go about this, including reduced teaching assignments for beginning teachers, formal induction programs, and encouraging teachers to grow into work with higher-need students. Donaldson (2005) highlights the experience of one differentiated career ladder that emphasizes not only ongoing learning and the incremental adoption of new responsibilities, but also decision making by master teachers who were well-respected by their peers. This program fosters and supports success among novice teachers while also honoring autonomy and control for more experienced veterans in the field.

Slow Down the Pace of Change

Lastly, some of the participating teachers' job insecurity came not from a faulty vision of reform, but rather from simply too much change happening too quickly. Liana felt that she enjoyed the challenges of teaching new content and addressing new student needs, but she would have liked the time to refine those skills before moving on to the next set. Miles saw a promising reform come and go within the space of one year. And Susan felt the need to selectively attend to reforms in order to create an environment that was best for her students. Some of their professional instability came not from the nature of the reforms, but simply from the excessive number of reforms.

Reform in education is a constant presence. Almost three decades ago, Cuban (1990) noted the continual cycle of school reform, commenting that many values-based, educational concerns could not be addressed through quick fixes. Other scholars of teacher professional development have reinforced this notion, demonstrating that extensive duration is needed for meaningful and lasting professional learning (Desimone et al. 2002) and that teacher development occurs along a continuum of many years (Feiman-Nemser 2001). Ongoing change is needed within education, but jumping from reform to reform too quickly undermines even valuable initiatives and eliminates them before they have the time to demonstrate their impact. This includes curriculum changes as well as school structures, openings, and closings. Slowing the pace of change in schools may also reduce the funds put toward reform, easing the budget to address other important needs.

Reflective Questions for Administrators

- What is my process for making hiring matches? Can it be evaluated and improved to promote stability for teachers?
- In what way(s) do I offer the teachers themselves genuine input into their teaching assignment?
- Do new hires and teaching assignments make effective use of educators' specialized skill sets?
- Do I provide support for novice teachers as they establish themselves in the field?
- What is the pace of change in my school? Is it sustainable?

Reflective Questions for Teacher Educators

- Do I facilitate with teacher candidates an understanding of the nuances of various teaching contracts? Do they understand what a temporary, permanent, and continuing contract represents?
- Do I explicitly develop the negotiating skills needed for beginning teachers to advocate for themselves on the teaching job market?
- Does my teacher preparation program develop specialized skills along with the breadth of expertise needed to fill vacant positions?

Suggested Readings for Administrators and Teacher Educators

Darling-Hammond, Linda, and Ann Lieberman. *Teacher Education around the World: Changing Policies and Practices*. New York: Routledge, 2012.

> This edited work describes some of the most effective education systems on the internationally based Programme for International Student Assessment (PISA); it includes chapters on Finland, Singapore, the Netherlands, United Kingdom, Hong Kong, Canada, and Australia. The editors note that a key commonality across all these systems is the "extent to which teaching has been organized and supported as a strong profession within these nations, with extensive investments in knowledge and skill."

(151). They argue for profession and capacity building through strong teacher preparation and professional development, induction models, and career ladders. This work may provide both administrators and teacher educators with concrete suggestions for enhancing the stability of the profession.

Johnson, Susan Moore, and the Project on the Next Generation of Teachers. *Finders and Keepers: Helping New Teachers Survive and Thrive in Our Schools.* San Francisco: Jossey-Bass, 2004.

This book describes a longitudinal study of the career pathways of fifty beginning teachers in Massachusetts. In particular, the authors capture the features that distinguish today's teachers from earlier generations, highlighting their broader professional options, increased emphasis on autonomy, and desire for a differentiated career path. The authors also note the importance of appropriate teaching assignments within a professional culture for promoting teacher success over time. They also highlight the misguided nature of a veteran-oriented culture that fails to address the needs of beginning educators. This piece provides an intriguing window into the perspectives of beginning teachers and their views on the profession.

Quartz, Karen Hunter, Brad Olsen, Lauren Anderson, and Kimberly Barraza Lyons. *Making a Difference: Developing Meaningful Careers in Education.* Boulder, CO: Paradigm Publishers, 2010.

This career handbook is targeted to an audience of preservice teachers. Its uniqueness lies in the way it makes explicit some of the implicit features of education, such as its low status and career cycle. The toolkit guides beginning teachers in thinking about how to make a difference through their careers, often steering them toward pathways with multiple stages, rather than a dichotomous choice of staying or leaving the classroom. It provides numerous opportunities for reflection and concrete tools to guide new teachers in shaping their own career journeys in ways that are meaningful to them. This handbook would enhance a student teaching seminar or early-career induction program.

Part III

**The Personal and the
Professional in
Teacher Attrition**

●●●●●●●●●●●●●●●●●●●●●●●

5

You Don't Fit Here

● ● ● ● ● ● ● ● ● ● ● ● ● ● ● ● ● ● ● ●

Teachers of Color
Coping with Racial
Microaggressions in Schools

Teachers of color are substantially underrepresented within the teaching force. The most recent statistics from the U.S Department of Education (2016) indicate that only 18 percent of the teaching population is comprised of people of color. Often teachers of color enter the profession with a desire to become change agents in the field (Lynn 2002; Mawhinney, Rinke, and Park 2012; Tolbert and Eichelberger 2016). There have been programmatic efforts to diversify the field (i.e., grow your own programs) by recruiting and retaining teachers of color, especially male teachers of color (Bryan and Browder 2013; Goings and Bianco 2016; Huntspon and Howell 2012; Lewis and Toldson 2013). Yet, these efforts have not been as successful as anticipated. Our study looks not at the overall statistics, but instead at the experiences of individual teachers of color working in schools, and it finds the prevalence of racial microaggressions to be central to their decisions to leave teaching.

This chapter reports on an unexpected finding from our study: the microaggressions and racial tensions experienced by teachers of color had both immediate and long-term impacts. We found that a majority of the teacher leavers of color shared very specialized experiences that incorporated racial dynamics in their teacher education programs and their interactions with school administrators. In order to provide a depth of narrative, we highlight the experiences of two of the teacher leavers, Abigail and Sasha, and the tensions they experienced around race. We chronicle the racial microaggressions Abigail and Sasha faced while teaching, but our goal is to use their counter-stories as a catalyst for broader discussions and reflections for teacher educators, administrators, and other stakeholders looking forward. We provide recommendations in order to promote dialogue around the role of race in the teaching profession.

Unpacking Microaggressions

Critical race theory (CRT) is a framework that uses race as the primary lens through which to view research data (Ladson-Billings 2001; Tate 1997; Wolfe 2011). One theoretical branch stemming from CRT is the concept of "microaggressions." Chester Pierce and colleagues (1978) first generated this theory within the field of counseling research. He coined the term "racial microaggressions" through his work around African Americans and the daily "subtle, stunning, often automatic exchanges which are 'put downs' of Blacks by offenders" (C. Pierce et al. 1978, 66). Sue and his colleagues (2007) further applied the term microaggressions to all of people of color, conceptualized as "brief, everyday exchanges that send denigrating messages to people of color because they belong to a racial minority group" (Sue et al. 2007, 273). The manifestation of these microaggressions can stem from individual racism, institutional racism, and cultural racism (Sue 2010).

Although the focus of microaggressions was initially around race, it is now acknowledged and considered to occur around gender (Barthelemy, McCormick, and Henderson 2016; Lester, Yamanaka, and Struthers 2016), sexual orientation (Francis and Reygan 2016), class (Q. Allen 2013), disabilities (Dávila 2015), language (Huber 2011), audist abilities (Stapleton and Croom 2017), or as is most often the case, an intersectionality of groups. Examples of intersectionality with microaggressions would be Stapleton and Croom's (2017) work exploring the microaggressions of Black d/Deaf college graduates (race/audist) or Dávila's (2015) work exploring Latinx special education students (race/ability/language). In short, microaggressions can occur and be directed at any marginalized group (Sue 2010) and the most vulnerable people in society (Berk 2017).

Sue (2010) explains that there are three forms, or taxonomy, of microaggressions: microinvalidation, microinsults, and microassaults. Microinvalidations are cues that exclude or invalidate the realities (i.e., feelings or thoughts) of marginalized peoples. This hurtful approach generally has four themes: (1) alien in own land (racial/ethnic minorities are foreigners), (2) color-blindness (denial of seeing color or race), (3) myth of meritocracy (race plays minor role in life), and (4) denial of individual racism. The second theme, microinsults, which is often the most common in situations where people tend to be rude or demean a person, contains four themes: (1) ascription of intelligence (connecting intelligence abilities to color or race), (2) second-class citizens (treat someone as lesser), (3) pathologizing cultural values/communication styles (values and communication for people of color are "lesser than"), and (4) assumption of criminal status (presumed criminal based on race). Lastly, microassaults are purposeful and intentional in nature. Microassaults are "explicit racial [, gender, or sexual orientation-based] derogation characterized primarily by a verbal or nonverbal attack meant to hurt the intended victim through name-calling, avoidant behavior, or purposeful discriminatory actions . . . they are most likely to be conscious and deliberate, although they are generally expressed in limited 'private' situations (micro) that allow the perpetrator some degree of anonymity" (Sue et al. 2007, 274). One element that makes microassaults so challenging is the psychic toll they take as the recipient weighs various responses. This psychic toll can become so great that, in the end, it can even drive a person from his or her chosen career, an experience captured by the teacher leavers highlighted in this chapter.

Felt but Not Seen: PreK–12 Teachers of Color Coping with Microaggressions

In the education world, microaggressions often act as gatekeepers (Wolfe 2011), denying teachers and students access, resources, and voice. Microaggressions are harmful with long-term impacts (Berk 2017) that can actively affect the workplace environment (DeCuir-Gunby and Gunby 2016). Numerous studies have explored the impact of microaggressions directed from teachers toward students in the PreK–12 sector (A. Allen, Scott, and Lewis 2013; Q. Allen 2013; Dávila 2015; Henfield 2011; Wolfe 2011), from the issue of mispronouncing students' names (Kohli and Solórzano 2012) to adaptive behaviors in the classroom (Andrews 2012). Research has also explored the effects of students' experiences with microaggressions in the higher education classroom (Barthelemy, McCormick, and Henderson 2016; Boysen 2012; Lester, Yamanaka, and Struthers 2016) and the campus environment (Hope, Keels, and Durkee 2016; Hotchkins 2016; Huber 2011; Smith et al. 2016; Suárez-Orozco et al. 2015).

Researchers have found that faculty of color in higher education settings face microaggressions more frequently than teachers in the PreK–12 sector (DeCuir-Gunby and Gunby 2016), often causing them to create faculty interest support groups to cope with these microaggressions (Follins, Paler, and Nanin 2015) or even leave higher education altogether (Chambers 2011/2012). This trend of microaggressions leading to career attrition is also prominent within university-based teacher preparation programs and PreK–12 schools. For example, Tolbert and Eichelberger (2016) chronicle the experiences of Sebina, a bilingual and biracial preservice teacher, who struggles with microaggressions and the attempted silencing of her voice from teacher education faculty and administration. Often Sebina's tussles were masked with the air of "social justice," although social justice was not actively practiced. Kraehe (2015) similarly chronicles the experiences of Brianna and Cherise, African American art education majors at a large predominately white institution (PWI). They experienced microaggressions in the program that pushed against their art-teacher identity and coped with the stark racial silence in the program.

Racialized microaggressions in the higher education setting also trickle down into the school setting for teachers of color. Endo (2015) discusses the longevity of these microaggressions, from preservice to in-service, among Asian American female teachers. In these instances, the intersectionality of microaggressions was present around race, gender (being sexualized), ethnicity (assumed not to be from the United States), and a struggle to survive within the "institution of whiteness." Similarly, African American classroom teachers experienced job dissatisfaction due to microaggressions (DeCuir-Gunby and Gundy 2016) because of continuous institutional tensions around race (Bryan and Browder 2013). Further, microaggressions are not limited to the U.S. context. Francis and Reygan (2016) explore the tensions that lesbian, gay, bisexual, and transgendered (LGBT) teachers faced with colleagues in South African schools.

The heartbreaking issue is that, despite the vital need for teachers of color in our classrooms, microaggressions are pushing potential educators of color out of the field. Goings and Bianco (2016) explored the perspectives of Black male students in a "grow your own" high school course designed to excite them about the teaching profession. Most of the participants expressed that they did not want to become teachers, as they too often experienced microaggressions as students and did not have enough (or any) teachers of color to serve as role models. Additional research shows that those who did want to teach and persevered eventually succumbed to racial battle fatigue from repeated microaggressions (Smith et al. 2016). This is why the stories presented in this chapter, or rather the counter-stories, are of such importance to understand this phenomenon.

Counter-narrative and Counter-storytelling

The storied experiences of teachers' lives pre-, in-, and post-career are essential for understanding how to recruit and sustain teachers of color. Schaefer, Downey, and Clandinin (2014) highlight the challenges of authentically representing the storied lives of white teacher leavers; such research is further complicated by the limited number and marginalization of teachers of color. For this reason, the counter-narrative is used to understand the construction of teacher identities (Tolbert and Eichelberger 2016), and as Kraehe (2015) explains, it can help to heal racial microaggressions. The counter-narrative is also referred to as counter-storytelling—"a critical race methodology [that]

Table 5.1
Former Teachers of Color Microaggressions in Their Career Life Histories

Teachers of Color	None	Microaggressions	
		Teacher training	Workplace
Abigail		X	X
Alicia		X	
Ayana	X		
Beatrice			X
Jennifer		X	
Lora			X
Nina			X
Sasha			X

provides a tool to counter deficit storytelling" (Solórzano and Yosso 2002). As the "majoritarian" story often reinforces privilege and can be another instrument of silencing, the counter-story is "a method of telling the stories of those people whose experiences are not often told (i.e., those on the margins of society). The counter-story is also a tool for exposing, analyzing, and challenging the marjoritarian stories of racial privilege. Counter-stories can shatter complacency, challenge the dominant discourse on race, and further the struggle for racial reform . . . within the histories and lives of people of color, there are numerous unheard of counter-stories. Storytelling and counter-storytelling these experiences can help strengthen traditions of social, political, and cultural survival and resistance" (Solórzan and Yosso 2002, 32). The teachers of color in this chapter, and specifically Abigail and Sasha, are counter-stories because they represent a voice not often heard in the literature, and they expose the issues of racial privilege in schools. It is in this vein that we present these stories of teacher leavers of color, in an effort to present the counter-stories that challenge and reshape the teaching workplace.

Counter-storytelling from Former Teachers of Color

The former teachers of color were all dedicated to the profession and frequently entered teaching in order to serve as advocates for students of color. The research shows that most teachers of color enter the profession in order to be change agents (Lynn 2002; Mawhinney, Rinke, and Park 2012). Yet, microaggressions played a large role in how the teachers of color constructed their career paths, interrupting their professional plans. All but one former teacher of color experienced some form of microaggression during their teacher training, at their workplace, or both (see table 5.1).

Table 5.2
Microinsult Themes in the Data

Themes	Microaggression	Message
Ascription of intelligence	"Why can't you do your paperwork like Ms. [Beatrice]?" Why aren't your students doing this like Ms. [Beatrice's] students are doing?"	All Asians are intellectually better
	"I mean when I tell you he [administrator] flew in that room, face was bright red. . . . I don't even know what to do about this situation. We [teacher and students] were all sort of just lost, kind of felt demeaned and it was just a horrible feeling."	Black Americans do an inferior job as teachers
Second-class citizen	"I felt like white students and white families and white people in general were treating Black folk like they didn't know science. And I was like, 'That's the devil.'"	Your kind does not belong here and you are not welcomed
	"I was the only African-American person in [teacher education program], and I was alienated and isolated. . . . I felt isolated. I felt ostracized. It was really bad, and then so in those moments, it was just isolating, and I decided, 'I'm not doing this,' and so I quit."	

These microaggressions may speak to the fact that the average number of years in the profession for teachers of color ($n = 8$) was only 4.8 years, compared to the white teachers ($n = 17$) at 8.1 years. Higher rates of attrition were often the result of numerous microaggressions, specifically microinsults, experienced by teachers of color. Table 5.2 displays selected quotes from the participants, the microaggression category, and the messages teachers received from these experiences.

Yet as evidenced by Abigail and Sasha's stories, these microaggressions were macro in their impact. We present here Abigail and Sasha's storied experiences, in this case counter-stories, in order to grasp the destructive power of microaggressions in teacher training and the workplace.

Abigail

Career Overview. Abigail is a Black teacher leaver who taught for two years in a mid-sized urban district on the East Coast. Growing up, Abigail went to public school in a major U.S. city. As she puts it, she led a "double life," studying regular academics during the day, and then attending an arts school for dance in the evening. Prior to attending university, Abigail traveled to Japan and South Africa to study languages and cultures. Even with Abigail's lifetime dedication to dance, she did not initially consider the arts for her future career.

Interestingly, she originally envisioned herself becoming a lawyer, but after being influenced by a college mentor, she set her sights on teaching: "[My mentor] said she always noticed that I had more of a teaching spirit. I was more so about making sure people were knowledgeable about themselves and what we were actually embarking on. So she thought that education was more so of a better route for me, being that I had just basically told myself, 'I'm gonna just go to law school,' knowing good and well I wasn't quite prepared to go down that road." Abigail followed her mentor's advice and decided to attend graduate school for her master's degree in English secondary education. The day after she finished her undergraduate degree, Abigail started graduate school. It was toward the end of her graduate program that Abigail experienced microassaults during her final field experience. As Abigail stated, "I ended up having a situation with one of my student teaching experiences that really kind of changed my perspective on things."

During this student teaching experience, Abigail taught in a school where the majority of the student body was African American. Her cooperating teacher was white, and Abigail perceived that she was threatened by how easily the students gravitated toward Abigail, "but she just made it up in their mind that basically I was trying to steal them away from her." According to Abigail, the tensions started to rise between the cooperating teacher and herself. It escalated into the following conversation: "Then the next thing I know, she's basically using my skin color as a way to say, 'Well, just because you're Black, it doesn't mean that you have a one-up. Basically, you can't use your skin color and your background to appeal to them.' I'm like, 'Okay, so where is this coming from? This is way left-field.' It really kind of put me in a different head-space." Eventually, this experience led to the cooperating teacher writing to the graduate school in an attempt to "blackball" Abigail from being able to obtain a position within the school district upon graduation. Abigail explained that the cooperating teacher "made it seem as though, 'Well, because she's Black, she's trying to appeal to the students' emotional side and making it so that they don't really get a realistic picture of what it means to be a student.'" But Abigail was determined to not let these instances affect her student teaching, so she "pressed forward."

Abigail worked with her students and planned a poetry slam "because I really wanted them to experience what we were doing in the class real-time." The poetry slam was held at a local Barnes & Noble, which donated half the proceeds back to the school. Moreover, the students also created all the promotional materials for the event, so they "really got a chance to learn that process." Abigail was committed to the students really utilizing and presenting authentic writing, but as for the cooperating teacher, "she just didn't like that." The cooperating teacher called Abigail's professor about the poetry slam "and just made it seem as though I was trying to hurt her or demean her or have it so that the students would go to the poetry slam and basically talk badly about their actual teacher. I was just like, 'I don't know about this whole teaching experience.' It just really put a sour taste in my mouth."

Pressing Forward and Getting Burned. Despite these feelings, Abigail continued to press forward, and shortly after her student teaching experience ended, she landed a teaching position at a new high school within the same school district. She was really excited about the position, as "all of the teachers were charged with laying the foundation and the framework of the school and making it the number-one spot [in the city]." Abigail was excited and committed to the school and the students. Because she had a background in dance and theater, she started an after-school program for students to continue their creative writing and couple it with the arts. During the after-school program, she and the students worked together to write a play, which they performed at events around the city.

After all this hard work, Abigail was surprised when she received her teaching evaluation from the white principal of the school: "I'll never forget, she actually said to me, 'I'm only hard on you because you're Black.'" . . . It crushed my spirit so much because I'm thinking as a new teacher on the block, I'm trying to come up with fresh stuff and trying to keep the students fully engaged." To make matters worse, Abigail discovered from her mentor at the school that "the principal wouldn't sign to approve me to be teacher of the year. She just felt as though that, '[Abigail] is doing too much.' And I said, 'Okay. I didn't know that you can get criticized or dinged for doing too much, whatever that's supposed to mean.'"

The following year, Abigail opted not to go back to that school. She had a friend who encouraged Abigail to try a charter school in the district, as the district had just hired a new Black principal who she heard was "doing great things." Abigail applied for the position and got the job. From the start, she started to notice that the white, male founder of the school had a "weird relationship" with the students. According to Abigail, "It was almost as if—I just have to be very blunt. It was almost as if he was the great white hope. He kind of fed the students with this idea that, 'All you've gotta do is come to school, and you'll be great.'"

Abigail continued to notice that the school founder maintained extremely low expectations for these African American students. She observed:

I noticed that over time that students were being rewarded for just very basic things like, "You came to school. Good job. Let's all go to see the new movie, *The Lorax*, because you came to school." I said, "Hold up. We haven't even addressed some of the basic things. The students need to learn this stuff so they can pass their exams. We need to be into it." It didn't matter to the founder.

The founder was pretty much like the dictator for the school. So if he said that everybody was going to go to the movie theater and didn't have any forewarning, everybody went to the movie theater.

These behaviors were complicated when Abigail started to notice that her students were "not up to par" with the seventh- and eighth-grade reading levels. Abigail was determined to do her job as a teacher and worked hard to promote student learning to the best of her ability.

Over time, the school's founder (not the principal) continually kept coming into Abigail's classroom. Worried about her past experiences, she thought to herself, "Now what is it? I'm not doing anything. I'm not trying to be a showoff. I'm just doing my job and handling business." The founder continued to come to her classroom and ask Abigail if she needed anything, to which she always replied she did not need anything: "And then I noticed that I had these random people that would just constantly come in my class. 'Oh my God, you're doing great things. You've got the students learning.' I'm at the point where I'm like, 'Okay, this is good. I'm getting some good feedback. Nobody's really making a fuss about what I'm doing, so maybe I'm doing a good job.' All of a sudden, it was like a 360."

At this point, the founder "turned his back" on Abigail, and he had rumors going around stating, "Well, [Abigail], she doesn't want help with anything. She wants to just do everything by herself," and very quickly Abigail found herself isolated from her peers and feeling on the outskirts of the social dynamic. But the issues stemmed deeper than Abigail being a "self-starter." She explained: "I come to find out what it was that he was intimidated because I suggested to him that some of the material that the students read is culturally relevant stuff. In order for me to get them to where they need to be, I need to make sure that the material is culturally relevant. He basically kind of frowned up like, 'Well, I don't really know what that is.'" Throughout the remainder of the school year, the situation with the founder of the school continued to be what Abigail described as "combative." Abigail finally stated to the founder. "You know what," she remarked, "I don't know if this is gonna work." Shortly afterward, she received a letter stating, "Thank you for your time here, but we don't need you to come back." It was at this point that Abigail decided, "I think I'm done with K–12. It was very political for me in terms of just trying to just teach."

During Abigail's student teaching and her two years within the profession, time and again she faced tensions around different racial perspectives on school and what is best for her majority-Black student body. Whether it was competition around relationships with students, undermining her hard work, or questioning her efforts to bring culturally relevant materials into the classroom, Abigail continually felt as if her perspective as a Black female teacher was undervalued: "Really it would just be the politics. Especially as a Black female, you already know about what it means to be educated. You understand what that is, and to have this knowledge and to be able to do what you need to do. . . . Every time that I did what I needed to do, I always got the results that I needed. When people tried to come in and change that, and from all of the political stuff that was going on, it just made it very hard, very frustrating, to do my job." It was the politics that racialized her career as a secondary teacher and led to her decision to leave the classroom.

Saturation Point. Abigail's decision to join the ranks of all the other teacher leavers did not go over well with her sorority sisters. Abigail belonged to a prominent Black sorority, and most of the sorority sisters lived in the city and worked as educators. "And so when they found out that I transitioned, it almost like World War III was happening, like, 'What, are you serious? Why aren't you doing this anymore?'" In essence, Abigail was criticized by her fellow Black educators for not sticking around, as there are so few Black teachers in the field. The pushback from her sorority sisters did have an impact. At one point, she said, "I felt really bad that I had made the decision, but I knew that I personally couldn't take it anymore because it [teaching] was making me a very angry person, and I didn't like that. I didn't like who I was becoming." The constant need to advocate for both herself and her students took its toll on Abigail emotionally. She felt it was time to move on from the classroom.

Abigail now teaches English at the community-college level. She also continues to work with youth in the performance arts realm, as she owns an African dance school. Abigail may still actively use her teaching skills in other educative areas, but her story of the racial struggle with administration has much to offer in terms of learning how to bridge the gap of race.

Sasha

Career Overview. Sasha is an Arab American who grew up in a large city. She attended private school in the city until the age of twelve, when her parents moved to the suburbs, as the expense of private education for both her and her brother was too costly. Aside from that fact, Sasha's neighborhood was becoming rampant with drugs, and after a drug-related murder happened two doors down, her parents decided that it was time to move out of the city. But Sasha's passion for the city sustained itself; she was a true outlier to our study because she was one of only two teacher leavers who wanted to be an urban teacher from the very beginning. Initially, her sights were on elementary education, but she found the courses lacked the challenge and rigor she enjoyed:

I always thought I wanted to be an elementary school teacher because I loved little kids and I loved working with them. It was such an exciting thing. Then when I would take these elementary ed. courses they were like painfully uninspiring. They were not uninspiring they were just not intellectually rigorous I felt like. I don't know if I consciously thought about this but I remember feeling like, "oh these courses are really lame." It wasn't really the same kind of intensive sort of academically rigorous experience that I was finding in my noneducation courses.

Sasha opted to change majors and study English secondary education with a minor in Africana studies instead: "I realized that I really loved literature and I loved writing and I would like to teach maybe Secondary English because those were very inspiring to me as well. So I shifted and I think—I don't know how consciously I thought of all of this stuff but I remember feeling like, 'oh this I like.' You know [to] take these courses that are easy passes, they were just not that interesting to me."

Sasha enjoyed her classes and graduated early from college. Unfortunately, graduating early made it problematic to find a teaching job, as the school year had already commenced. She found a job working for a nonprofit organization in the interim: "I got this job at a nonprofit working with youth in these projects in [a neighborhood]. Actually really liked it except the administration changed and they started firing all of these people who were really awesome people, so finally I quit because it was just became this really awful environment."

After the nonprofit experience ended, it was closer to the start of a new school year, and Sasha got a job at a high school in the district. Although Sasha had a wonderful student teaching experience during her teacher training, her first job in the district was a very different experience. She admitted, "I really liked my students a lot; they were really great. But the school was a mess. It was like everybody—teachers just constantly yelling at students, administrators yelled at teachers, there was this sense of threat over us." The experience in this school quickly came to a halt. In January, due to budget issues, Sasha was excessed (laid off) from the school: "I got a notice that I was excessed 'cause I was the least senior teacher. It was me and a few other people. There were other teachers who were as low on the ladder as I was but they were in alternative cert. programs they couldn't excess those people because those alternative cert. programs had a deal." The school continued to keep Sasha on as a substitute teacher.

Yet there happened to be an opening at the school where Sasha had completed her student teaching—a small, alternative school with a healthy population of immigrant children, many of whom were Latinx. The school contacted Sasha specifically to fill an opening in tenth-grade humanities, which she accepted. "They really liked me there [at the school]," Sasha said, "and they just didn't have a job for me when I started teaching but they had an opening suddenly, they just happened to have an opening, and they called me up and they were like 'Do you want to come and work for us?' I was like 'Yes please get me out of here.' They heard that I was excessed." Sasha transitioned into teaching ninth-grade social studies the following year, while also becoming team leader. She was not certified in social studies, but the school did not have an open English position. It was during this time that Sasha experienced a number of racial incidents with the administration.

In the Face of Activism. One of Sasha's administrators was José, a Puerto Rican principal of this alternative school. In the beginning, Sasha and José had a good working relationship: "He loved me. He used to say all this stuff about my classroom, how great it was, and all this stuff." The relationship worked, although José's leadership style juxtaposed that of the school's foundational ideals:

> He had a more authoritarian leadership style and he was in a school that had been established more as a very democratic space: where both teachers and students had a lot of say, there was a lot of emphasis on student voice and on teacher leadership and because it was a small environment teachers had a lot of leadership roles and were constantly doing stuff. . . . He espoused all of these sort of progressive ideals but the way he led was not that way. Everybody kind of had issues with him; he was annoying and he didn't like the teachers who spoke out and stuff.

Over the second year of Sasha's teaching, this relationship started to change. This was catalyzed by the World Trade Center attack on September 11, 2001. The school was a mere two miles away from the occurrence. She recalled, "When it happened it was a big deal; it affected us very directly because we were right in the middle of Manhattan and there was this really—it was so complex how we were supposed to dismiss students and we were concerned that students had family members there and stuff. I don't remember having any students who lost anybody but there were definitely students whose parents worked right around the World Trade Center and stuff. It was this really intense thing." This incident would become a focal point for the differential racial experiences between Sasha and her administration. In the days following the attack, the Federal Bureau of Investigation (FBI) visited Sasha's cousin, who is a Moroccan immigrant. Sasha's family started to get nervous, so she asked José, "'Look, I'm Arab, my cousin just got this visit from the FBI, and I need to just go home for the weekend. Can I take a few days off and just go home and be with my family for the weekend?' So I did and he was fine with it."

A few months following this incident, Sasha's students were doing a business project within the local community. Local businesses would lead workshops with the students, and some of the community members suggested the students make and sell American flag pins. Sasha, an antiwar activist, had other students in the class who were also against the idea of war. Thus, the students suggested making peace signs instead of American flag pins. Sasha noted, "These corporate guys were like 'What? How could you say that?' and [the students] are like, 'Yeah the ones [peace pin] that Ms. [Sasha] wears.' And [the corporate guys] were like, 'What this is terrible!' and they sort of alerted the administration . . . and basically the administration started coming down hard on me and started saying 'You can't brainwash the kids.' I was like who's brain washing who?"

Following this incident, the school started a new mandatory policy requiring all students and school personnel to recite the pledge of allegiance. Sasha stated:

> I don't believe in pledging allegiance to any flag, especially not the American flag. I didn't say it and I didn't tell my students what to do but I did not stand for the pledge of allegiance and I refused to make my students stand as well. I told them, "You have the choice to do whatever you want." And I brought in a handout because it became an issue; the administration was telling them they had to. It became—I brought in a handout that detailed a bunch of Supreme Court cases that said that they have the freedom to do whatever they want.

Then the issue with the pledge of allegiance came to a head: "The assistant principal, who was this white guy, and he was actually had a doctorate in ethics interestingly enough; he came in and was like 'You have to pledge allegiance, you have to stand up for the pledge of allegiance and you have to pledge allegiance. It's not—you're not allowed to not.' I was like, 'Actually no they have the right to do whatever they want.' The principal and the assistant principal came in and they were screaming at me in front of the kids." It got to the point where the administration would come in and yell at the students to stand for the pledge of allegiance, and on their own accord, all the students would spontaneously sit down in silent protest. But the protest was in response to administration's treatment of Sasha. They would not say the pledge "only because I was being attacked. It wasn't really a political stance in the sense of being—they didn't have—they actually probably would have all pledged allegiance."

Eventually the administration would call students and their parents into the office if they were wearing a pin with a peace symbol. "They were clearly on the attack and they were clearly attacking me . . . and they couldn't attack me based on my teaching 'cause actually my students were learning a lot and I was successful as a teacher." The attacks continued in small, minute ways. For example, Sasha had the students bring in different foods connected with each student's background, something that she called "ridiculously simplistic."

The administration would write Sasha up for having the students bring in food because it was "going off the curriculum."

Ultimately, the administration figured out a way to get rid of Sasha. At first, "they didn't have any reason to excess [layoff] anybody except that they were allowed to excess people if they had too many people under one certification and not enough under another certification. So they used that to excess me. It was totally all of us could see it coming." Sadly, the administration planned the timing of the news in a way that prevented Sasha from being able to say good-bye to her students. In short, Sasha said, "It was so fucked up."

When Sasha was asked directly if this situation grew as complex and tense as it did because she is Arab, she replied, "Yeah, I think being Arab was very big part of it." With that and Sasha's activism, she advocated for herself and went to the city's union to appeal the excessing decision. The union assigned Sasha to a union representative outside of her school to bring forth the case. Sasha explained the union representative's advice as follows: "He was Armenian, and he said to me 'You know what? This is a losing cause. You're going to lose this right now. You're going to lose this hearing. I wouldn't even bother appealing. There's nobody in the Board of Ed. that it going to hear you on this. You have a case, you're right, you're totally right, but you just don't even bother. You're gonna end up spending a lot of time for nothing.' He was nice, and he did his best. He wasn't being a jerk. He was just giving me the honest truth about it."

Sadly, the union representative was correct, and Sasha lost the case. But, luckily, a friend in Sasha's professional network was able to get her a teaching job at another alternative school in the city where he was a teacher. Eventually, Sasha moved back to the city she grew up in and taught there. She taught at a charter school, where she also struggled with issues of race and the treatment of teachers—so much so, in fact, that all the teachers in a specific program housed in the school staged a massive walkout. Everyone decided to resign together, and the teachers actually shut down the program. Sasha never went back to teaching within the K–12 schools again. Her story, like Abigail's, clearly illustrates that differential experiences of race and ethnicity played a big role in shaping teachers' career trajectories, within and ultimately out of the classroom.

Lessons from Storied Experiences

We certainly are not highlighting Abigail's and Sasha's stories to argue that all teachers of color will have different racialized experiences than their administrators or to showcase an "us versus them" mentality. But, Abigail's and Sasha's experiences as teachers of color offer a valuable lesson in the important and often silent role of racial dynamics in the teaching profession. Frequently in education, we discuss the critical role that race plays in students' experiences, including culturally relevant/responsive pedagogy, multicultural curriculums, and implicit bias. But very little is spoken about the differential racial experiences of educators themselves.

This also becomes apparent when we examine the experiences of white teachers working with majority students of color. For example, our participant Amber, a white female, taught English at a school with almost exclusively students and teachers of color (mainly African American and Latinx). Amber was one of two white teachers in the building. Often times, she would be left out of teacher and administrator gatherings that occurred inside and outside the school. "It was such an insular community, and I was so clearly an outsider, and that was made evident to me on an almost daily basis." Moreover, she often lacked administrator support. For example, she had a parent-teacher conference with a mother who was hostile toward Amber. The parent said to Amber: "I'm just gonna tell you his dad doesn't like white people. He really hates white people and he's kind of teaching him like that same belief. So that's just what it is. I mean I'm sorry, but there's really not much you can do about it. He really picked that up from his dad, and he doesn't like white people either now. So you know, that's why he's treating you like that." Amber was at a loss for how to respond to this parent. She explained, "You're telling me I can't teach your son because I'm white and I don't know where to go from there." She did not feel supported when she shared this dilemma with the administration. Eventually, Amber said, "I reached a point where I felt like I can't be an effective teacher in this environment, in this context, and it's just time for me to go." In Amber's situation, we also see how different racial experiences come into play. Once again, Amber's experience highlights the need for administrators to explicitly discuss differential racial experiences and help teachers from all backgrounds work through racial tension that might emerge within and outside of the classroom.

Abigail and Sasha were two teachers who were very dedicated to their profession. They really seemed to love the teaching. However, the outside influences and microassaults became too much of a burden for them to remain in the teaching profession long term. In the following section, we offer some suggestions to help teacher educators and administrators (re)build the relationships between teachers and staff, particularly administrators and staff from different racial and ethnic backgrounds.

Recommendations

The counter-stories of Abigail, Sasha, and the rest of the former urban teachers of color show the powerful and detrimental role of racial microaggressions within the teaching profession. While we often consider the role of race in the lives and experiences of preK–12 students, these dynamics are similarly influential in the lives of teachers, often playing a role in teachers' decisions to leave the classroom. This is quite damaging to efforts to construct a more diverse teaching profession that reflects that racial makeup of U.S. students.

It is evident that to truly encourage people of color to enter and remain within the teaching profession, we must use counter-stories to move teacher education and the workplace forward. Mellor (2004) argues that teachers of color require the ability to cope with microaggressions beyond the daily emotional experiences and circumstances. In other words, the profession, as a whole, needs to work toward the elimination of racial microaggressions. The "discourse regarding equity and inclusivity must go beyond committee meetings, cultural celebration months, and mission statements. These things can supplement an inclusive campus [and school workplace] but cannot make up for one that does not practice inclusiveness, particularly when it really matters" (Stapleton and Croom 2017, 25). Here we provide recommendations for teacher training and the workplace by utilizing these counter-stories to push the profession forward. We urge teacher educators and administrators not to simply ignore racial dynamics taking place in their educational institutions but instead to identify and, if needed, bring these undercurrents out into the open so that preservice and in-service teachers do not feel alone and can process them in emotionally healthy ways that lead to success, support, and retention in the field.

The Workplace and Administrators

Abigail's, Sasha's, and Amber's experiences all show the power of administrators and others in position of power, when microaggressions are an intricate part of the working experience. Past research has shown that principals, and the supports they offer, directly influence how teachers see their teaching practice, and more broadly, how they see themselves (Littrell et al. 1994). Johnson, Kraft, and Papay (2012) identify nine key elements to quality work environments for teachers, and one of these elements is the principal. Over the decades, new accountability policies for students as well as teachers have put more influence on school leadership for the success, and even survival, of schools (S. Pierce 2014). In short, the influence of the "intrinsic empowerment of the workplace" on teachers' job satisfaction is intimately connected (Davis and Wilson 2000) to the principal. But when microaggressions come from administrators, most teachers of color will eventually leave their posts, or even the profession altogether.

Our recommendations for teacher educators also apply to administrators in making a more conducive workplace. In addition, there are programs, such as the National School Reform Faculty (www.nsrfharmony.org), that have developed what are known as Critical Friends Groups ® (CFGs), which can support administrators in discussing race and illuminating microaggressions. These groups are originally situated for groups of 8–12 teachers to gather and develop their skills by using protocols to enhance their instruction. CFGs have also been used with groups of administrators to help build leadership skills and provide support, avoiding the all-too-common experience of isolation. A CFG would be the ideal setting in which administrators can start reflecting on the role that race plays in their school, for students as well as faculty. The National School Reform Faculty offers a variety of freely available protocols on their website, and many can be used effectively around issues of race, as well as many other topics of equity and diversity.

Administrators and teachers can also find much-needed support outside the school buildings by making use of the benefits of technology. Facebook has sprouted a number of support groups for teachers of color, who may benefit from hearing stories similar to their own. For example, the Facebook group "Black Educators Rock!!!" has a following of over 150,000 people. This has become a safe space for teachers of color to support each other with ideas, humor, or dialogue about and around the classroom.

Teacher Training and Teacher Educators

Reflecting the work of Tolbert and Eichelberger (2016) and Kraehe's (2015) counter-stories, Abigail's counter-storied experience is evidence that teachers of color encounter detrimental microaggressions during their teacher training. Racial silencing and ignoring race in teacher preparation are not conducive to building an inclusive climate (Kraehe 2015). On the contrary, it is important to incorporate and have candid discussions around race. This essentially starts with the teacher educator himself/herself. We also strongly recommend that teacher educators take explicit steps to gain cultural competence in working with educators from backgrounds different from their own. Reading and attending workshops about white privilege, racial identity development, implicit bias, and microaggressions can help educational leaders of all sorts to better comprehend the differential and often-contentious racial dynamics experienced by teachers of color.

Engaging in reflective conversations with colleagues about different racial-ized experiences in U.S. society and becoming comfortable acknowledging and expressing emotions related to race could go a long way in promoting a common understanding. Specifically, DeCuir-Gunby and Gunby (2016) discuss the importance of "teaching how to cope with racism while actively working for change and helping students [preservice teachers] on how to deal with racial microaggressions while in the workplace" (407). A. Allen and colleagues (2013) add that making culturally affirming education central to the teaching approach and racial consciousness of a classroom will go far in starting to break the barriers of microaggressions. In order to facilitate these discussions, the leading expert in microaggressions, Sue (2016), created a resource that argues for the critical importance of discussing race openly, and it offers concrete suggestions for doing so, even in a resistance climate.

Essentially, Wolfe (2011) argues for microtransformations, where in the classroom the teacher's pedagogical practice is embedded with small (or micro) interactions "that create student subjectivities allowing for wider access to resources . . . different interactions or discourse processes on the part of teacher and students can hold the possibility of positively transforming students' racialized subjectivities" (80). The following questions can help teacher educators reflect on how to encourage microtransformations in their university classrooms.

Reflective Questions for Administrators

- What experiences have I had related to race in my work in schools? How might someone with a different background have experienced work life differently? Have I taken concrete steps to foster an environment where teachers and staff can discuss/dialogue about race in an easy and effective manner?
- What supports have I put in place to make myself reflective and accountable about my approach to all teaching and staff members?
- What are my underlying beliefs, attitudes, and assumptions around race? How do these play into my leadership style?

Reflective Questions for Teacher Educators

- What experiences have I had related to race in my work with preservice teachers? How might someone with a different background have experienced schooling/education differently? Have I taken concrete steps to foster an environment where preservice teachers can discuss/dialogue about race in an easy and effective manner?
- How do I process issues of race with my preservice teachers' field experiences? What is a safe and effect way to do this to support the students in their classrooms and your own classroom?
- When a preservice teacher is faced with a racial microassault (e.g., Abigail's incident with her cooperative teacher), what procedures are in place to help protect the preservice teacher?

Suggested Readings for Administration and Teacher Educators

Sue, Derald Wing. *Race Talk and the Conspiracy of Silence: Understanding and Facilitating Difficult Dialogues on Race.* Hoboken, NJ: John Wiley & Sons, 2016.

Sue, a national expert on multicultural psychology, offers background on why it is so difficult to raise dialogues about race, particularly in a classroom setting. He offers concrete suggestions of how and why to have critical discussions on race within and outside the classroom. This book is a great tool for administrators and teacher educators who are trying to do the same within their school and workplace environments.

Singleton, Glenn E. *Courageous Conversations about Race: A Field Guide for Achieving Equity in Schools*. New York: Corwin Press, 2014.

This second, updated edition of the original book is a great tool for administrators. It was originally designed for educators to understand inequality in school curriculum, but it is loaded with many tools on how to talk about race and have an open dialogue with teaching staff and preservice teachers. There is also a supplemental facilitator's guide handbook that can also be purchased for administrators' and teacher educators' use.

Berlak, Ann, and Sekani Moyenda. *Taking It Personally: Racism in the Classroom from Kindergarten to College*. Vol. 8. Philadelphia: Temple University Press, 2001.

This book is well suited for teacher educators. It starts out with Moyenda, an African American elementary teacher, coming into Berlak's higher education classroom as a guest speaker. What is chronicled is an intense dialogue and examination about race. Although this is an older book, Lynnette has taught with this book before, and it has been a powerful piece with preservice teachers. The book still discusses up-to-date issues on race.

6

Negotiating Gendered and Cultural Expectations on a Teacher's Salary

●●●●●●●●●●●●●●●●●●●●●

The Mediating Role of Identity

It is commonly accepted that teaching is not a highly paid pursuit. Hoyle (2001) actually categorizes it as a semiprofession, thus conveying its lower status and prestige than other occupations. This semiprofessional view of teaching, coupled with its largely female workforce, has resulted in a chronically underpaid field. Moreover, the culture of education socializes teachers to communicate their motivation as being related to intrinsic factors, such as interacting with children and making a difference, rather than the seemingly superficial extrinsic factors of salary and benefits. Lortie's (1975) foundational work on teacher socialization demonstrates that teachers prioritize psychic rewards over material ones, and more recent studies of teacher professional motivations (e.g., Olsen 2008; Watt et al. 2012) demonstrate that very little has changed in the intervening years.

Research on the career development effects of salary is mixed, indicating that salary is not of primary importance, but rather one of many factors influencing teachers' careers over time. As we previously mentioned, work on teachers' motivations for entering and remaining in the field largely focuses on their sense of mission and direct work with students (e.g., Brunetti 2006; Nieto 2005). However, teachers are not entirely satisfied with their salaries. Sixty-four percent of active teachers who responded to the MetLife Survey on the American

Teacher (Markow, Macia, Lee, and Harris Interactive 2013) reported a lack of satisfaction with the teaching salary. Related work demonstrates that wages are important to teachers' decisions to enter the field (Bacolod 2007b), that teachers earning higher salaries are less likely to move between schools (Garcia, Slate, and Delgado 2009), and teachers with higher starting salaries are more likely to persist in the classroom over time (Gray and Taie 2015). Nevertheless, some teacher leavers have indicated greater satisfaction with their careers outside the classroom, even when their salaries are lower (Buchanan 2009).

Rather than salary having a fixed or predetermined effect on teachers' career decisions, it seems that instead the influence of salary is mediated by identity. Clandinin and colleagues (2015) conceptualize teacher attrition as an identity-making process, and our work reflects this approach across the professional life span. Chapter 1 illustrated the ways in which the broader societal context outside of the school building shaped teachers' perceptions of salary and prestige, chapter 2 highlighted the interaction with specific administrators and the larger educational system, and chapter 5 emphasized the impact of differential racialized experiences in schools. In this chapter, we further explore this notion, illustrating the ways in which teachers' societal experiences with gender and culture, in particular, mediate their perception of and decisions related to salary. We share some of the participating teacher leavers' discontent with salary, particularly their long-term salary expectations, and we highlight two case studies of teachers struggling with gendered and cultural expectations related to salary.

Overall Influence of Salary

The research literature indicates that salary is one among many factors affecting teachers' career decisions. The life histories from our pool of teacher leavers reflects the same theme. As sometimes believed, salary was not an overriding influence for teachers leaving the classroom. Nevertheless, it did represent an important factor for a substantial minority of teacher leavers. Among our sample, only 24 percent of the teacher leavers discussed salary as at least one aspect of their rationale for leaving. This number may be artificially decreased because of the social norm that teachers are motivated by intrinsic factors; that is, some participants may not have felt comfortable publicly discussing the role of salary in their career decisions.

Rather than viewing salary as just a single pay rate, Imazeki (2002) instead outlines three types of wages that can influence teachers' behavior: current salary, expected salary in the district, and relative wage. It seems that all three types of wages influenced teachers' decision making. For instance, Monica shared her discontent with her current salary, noting, "I work 100 hours a week, I repeat myself every day, and I can't afford to go on vacation." She expressed dissatisfaction with her ability to live the lifestyle she wanted on her current salary. On the other hand, Liana shared her desire for more room to grow professionally, noting, "There's just not really anywhere for me to go either in terms of more responsibility or more pay." Liana's experiences reflect Imazeki's notion of expected salary.

Finally, there were other teachers who compared the teaching salary to their opportunities outside the field of education. For instance, Patricia left teaching to pursue a doctoral program in chemical oceanography. In making her decision, she reasoned that a graduate student's salary was not too far from a teacher's salary, explaining, "Financially, I'm very lucky that going to grad school in a STEM field, your tuition is paid for and you get a stipend, which honestly, is a pay cut from teaching, but it wasn't super drastic given how little I was making." Her low teaching salary actually made it easier for Patricia to transfer back to life as a student. Other teacher leavers were shocked at their own earning potential. Jordan noted that she made more money as a first-year computer programmer than in nine years as a classroom teacher. Patricia's and Jordan's experiences reflect Imazeki's (2002) notion of relative wage, illustrating once again how education does not exist in isolation, but must in all realms, including salary, compare itself against other career sectors.

In the following section, Andrew's and Alicia's storied experiences emphasize the role of salary in their decisions to leave teaching. In particular, these cases illustrate that it is not salary alone, but the mediating role of identity in perceiving and evaluating salary that appears to make a difference for teachers.

Andrew

Career Overview. Growing up with a firefighter-father and paramedic-mother in the South, Andrew described everyone in his family as working in a service profession with a "verb plus—er kind of job." He explained, "One of the things I really liked about being around my family was that they all had a sort of service-type career in the sense, they were helping people and it seemed really noble and idealistic." After a circuitous career that included international contracting and accounting for a prominent aerospace firm, a lingering feeling of lacking professional fulfillment, of having a good job but not being able to name exactly what he did, bothered Andrew. Andrew noted the connection back to the service professions, explaining, "It was kind of like a really strong family thing . . . and I always liked the idea of teaching."

When he broached the subject with his wife at the time, Andrew's wife resisted a move to teaching because of the material benefits of his current job. According to Andrew: "She flips out because to her it's a huge step backwards professionally speaking. I've got a job. It's stable. It's not fun but we're able to pay our mortgage and we've got a car. It's comfortable. . . . This is a pretty good job, why are you so dismissive of it?" Eventually Andrew and his then-wife parted ways, and Andrew saw his opportunity to make a career change. He saw an advertisement online for an alternative certification program on the East Coast and decided to apply, explaining, "I was really excited. [Teaching] had everything. It's like the romance of making a difference. I get to do something positive and socially fulfilling with the work that I'm doing. I can support myself." Thrilled with the prospect of becoming a teacher, Andrew left the South to become a science teacher.

During and after his completion of the program, Andrew worked at a school focused on serving immigrant students and English language learners, and he thrived in that environment for almost a decade. Andrew explained: "I really love[d] my work. I liked what I was doing. I felt good about it. I got recognized for it. I won a prize for classroom excellence. . . . I got a letter from Bill Clinton. He's like, 'Hey, I read about you in the newspaper. I think you're really great.'" Andrew had no doubts about his career change and his work with students.

Struggling Financially. Although Andrew thrived professionally during this time, he struggled personally. While working as a teacher, Andrew had remarried and was now the father of two young children. But he did not feel that he could adequately support his family. Recalling his financial difficulties, he remarked, "We're just always getting by. It's never huge progress. We'll have a rare splurge. We'll get to a point where there'll be a spasm of, 'I just can't take this frugal stuff anymore' and then we'll take a trip or something, but it's just not sustainable."

Andrew felt that surviving on a teacher's salary in a major city, with a wife who stayed home with the children, was simply an impossible situation. He explained: "Frankly, the financial reality of paying—of having two kids at that point, it was almost, given what she was making, it didn't really make a lot of sense for her to keep working either. It's really hard to support your family just being a teacher if both of you aren't working especially." He realized that he had to make a change. Not wanting to leave teaching altogether, Andrew began to consider going into school administration: "I was desperate a little bit because I really wanted to stay in the school environment. I really liked what I was doing. I knew that this was something that I was potentially going to have to do. And so my proposition was, 'Hey, listen, if I become an administrator, I get to stay in school. I get to keep going in my career.' I don't really want to leave it. I like the people that I work with. I like the kids." Reasoning that it would be a sacrifice, but would allow him to support his family while continuing to work with schools and students, Andrew entered a principal-training program.

From Teacher to School Administrator. While completing his training, Andrew became the principal of a school and once again found professional, but not personal, success. Feeling a deep responsibility for his students and teachers,

Andrew devoted every spare minute to supporting his school. He worked 11–12-hour days, twelve months a year, explaining, "It's been super, super hard. My wife barely saw me last year. . . . It has just really sucked a lot out of me." Although he was making more money as a school principal, Andrew felt as if he was continually slipping behind because he was also taking on new responsibilities. He explained: "I was in a better position when I came up here [to the Northeast] ten years ago. I was financially not as bad off as I am now when I had half as much education. But it's really hard because I don't feel like I have anything to show personally for sort of this big sacrifice, and when it's just me and my wife it's one thing. Now that I've got kids, it's like we're not saving for college. Like this is really screwed up." Andrew reflected further on the challenges of supporting a family: "Frankly, the money is not—like I just assumed it was going to solve all my problems. I'm going to make so much money. It sounds like a lot of money until you start making it. . . . I'm pulling down a bigger paycheck personally, but because it's being divided out across more people, it just doesn't feel like much, and there's no prospect that we're ever going to own anything up here because we just can't get ahead." Although he sacrificed for a larger paycheck, he still felt unable to keep up.

Andrew's mother-in-law came to live with them for a while to help with childcare while Andrew was deep into the start-up of his new position. However, she could not handle life in the city and moved home. Sadly, his wife soon followed: "She moved back. She couldn't take it anymore. . . . It's not like she and I are having problems or anything but just the stress of being alone with the kids. . . . Yeah, I'm making more money but it's kind of that weird dynamic because it's more money than I've ever made before. And, yet, I'm trying to support four people off of it, so I feel as broke as I've ever felt." Andrew envisioned a few possible scenarios moving forward. He imagined his wife might return to work once the children were a little older, and his position was more secure. He saw a potential move to be with them in the South, where the cost of living is lower but the salaries are comparatively lower. Or he might earn more with a new principal's contract. But for now he noted, "I'm worried about it. I'm really worried about it."

Alicia

Career Overview. Growing up in a suburban community on the East Coast, Alicia always worked with children, volunteering at summer Bible programs and helping her mother with children she watched in their home. So it was a natural fit that when Alicia went to college, she would pursue a teaching degree. Alicia explained: "I was accepted and enrolled in [the university]. I decided right then and there that teaching would be my major because number one, I enjoyed kids and working with kids. Number two, my parents thought it was a good profession for a girl. And number three, I just, outside of that I wasn't sure of what I would be good at or what I would be interested at and my parents wanted me to choose a major then and there." Moreover, Alicia shared that her parents held what she termed "traditionally Asian views" about work and marriage. They believed that a woman should not prioritize her career because she would be taken care of financially by her husband while she cared for the children. "They had pushed me into teaching originally because they felt it was a good profession for females," Alicia said. "They had this thing, part of the Asian culture, that I would marry early and be taken care of from a money standpoint. They weren't too concerned about the profession." Not fully aware of her alternatives, Alicia agreed to follow her parents' direction and become a teacher.

Lingering Career Doubts. Once in the classroom, Alicia found teaching to be exceptionally hard work. She initially struggled during student teaching because of personality conflicts with her mentor teacher. This was followed by the challenging task of taking over a classroom in a Title I school mid-year. It was a classroom in which students were dealing with "homeless shelters, abuse, anger. . . . They were stealing my scissors and fashioning them into knives. And this was first grade." Discouraged by the obstacles she faced in teaching students the academics, Alicia commented, "Nobody in teaching seems to tell you that it's hard." Although she was exhausted and disillusioned, her vice principal encouraged her to stick with it. Alicia recalled: "I remember the vice principal telling me that I wasn't really going to get into, you know, I really wasn't gonna feel like I was in the rhythm of things until my second or third year of teaching, which was true. I got better and better. By the third year I was pretty much used to, you know, it wasn't affecting me, I wasn't crying basically all the time." Alicia overcame the initial challenges and stayed in teaching for four and a half years, even earning a master's degree in STEM education, a field that was initially intimidating to her.

Although Alicia improved and became more comfortable in the classroom setting, she still held lingering doubts about her career choice. Alicia explained, "From the beginning I was always questioning my decision. [Sometimes] I enjoyed teaching and sometimes I hated teaching and I just was never, ever sure." In terms of professional growth, she noted, "It feels like a dead end." Plus, "I was struggling mentally and that was a concern."

In addition to doubts about career fit, Alicia also grappled with the challenges of supporting herself on a teacher's salary: "From a money standpoint I was living from paycheck to paycheck while being very frugal and I envisioned myself, you know, I'd look at the schedule, I mean I'd have to be working fifteen to twenty-five years before I could even make it, while paying out of pocket for so many things. I just couldn't see how I could live comfortably on this, in this profession." Her financial struggles, together with what Alicia termed "the sacrifices involved," eventually pushed her to begin looking for other opportunities.

Finding a New Career Path. Alicia knew that she was ready to start looking for other career opportunities, but she did not have a firm career path in mind. "It didn't really matter so much what it was," she remarked, "I just wanted to get my foot into the door of the corporate world. I had a sense that perhaps there were areas, skill sets, that I might be strong in that I didn't realize." Having completed an education major and four and a half years in the classroom, she also knew that she did not have a "coherent story" that would translate for hiring managers in other fields. So she decided to take what she called a "back door" strategy and started networking, both face-to-face and on social media. She remarked, "I told everyone that I was looking."

Although Alicia did not have experience outside of education, eventually someone knew someone who was looking for a support person at a staffing company, and Alicia got the job. She recalled that at first the work was largely administrative, but over time she proved herself and moved up the ladder, first into a senior recruiting position and later into a management and training role. Alicia also enjoyed the flexibility of her new schedule, noting, "There was a lot of autonomy and even the little things that a lot of people take for granted, like being able to go to the restroom or taking a coffee break. You know, office supplies were provided without me having to spend money out of pocket." However, one of the most satisfying aspects of her new job was the salary. She commented, "I knew that teachers were underpaid, but it really hit home to me after I left and I was making so much more money."

Alicia even succeeded in convincing her parents that she had made a good career move. Although they had originally encouraged her to go into teaching, they now saw that she could be successful in another field. Alicia explained: "They had some fears because the recruiting and staffing world is generally volatile. It's very metrics-driven so if you don't earn production figures, you're out the door and they were worried about that. But I reassured them because I'm very competitive, so they were fine with it." Although Alicia misses her students, she does not feel that she can ever go back to teaching, noting, "No matter how much harder I work, and no matter how hard I work in recruiting, like 14-hour days, nothing comes close to the amount of cognitive/mental/emotional effort that came from teaching."

Gender and Cultural Mediation of Teacher Salaries

The experiences of these teacher leavers reveal that although salary is often not the sole reason for leaving teaching, it is nevertheless an important factor to consider in shaping teachers' careers. Almost one-quarter of the participating teacher leavers cited salary as a factor in their decisions, and that number was probably deflated because of social norms around teaching. Some teachers, like Andrew, cited income as the primary reason for a career move, and others, like Alicia, grew weary of the constant struggle to make ends meet. Their life histories indicate that low teaching salaries do indeed drive teachers out of the profession.

Gendered Mediation

The lived experiences of these teacher leavers also highlight the important notion that salary does not necessarily reflect a direct, cause-and-effect relationship with retention. Instead, teachers' perceptions of salary are mediated by their identities. One aspect of identity that appears to have a strong mediating relationship with salary is gender. Although the majority of families in the United States bring in two incomes, men are nevertheless still considered the family "breadwinners." Traditional notions of family view men as the primary wage earners, even as contemporary notions also compel them to share in the running of the household (Families and Work Institute 2007).

In contrast, over the last century classroom teaching has been overwhelmingly women's work (Biklen 1995). Historically, teaching was largely feminized in the late 1800s during the expansion of compulsory secondary schooling, and it became one of the few "respectable" professions available to women (Clifford 1989, 305). Perhaps because of its largely female workforce, teaching has also held low status and accompanying low pay (Hoyle 2001). It was seen as a profession to accompany mothering; female teachers were viewed as nurturers (Clifford 1989), and teacher attrition was attributed to changing family needs (Maher and Ward 2002).

The feminization of the profession has consequently reduced its appeal for men. Fewer men express interest in teaching, citing status, salary, and a predominantly female work environment as primary factors influencing their decision (Cushman 2005). In today's workforce, slightly over three-quarters of all public classroom teachers are women (National Center for Education Statistics 2016) and 84 percent of elementary teachers are female (Papay 2007). Moreover, once in the classroom, men are more likely to leave (Gray and Taie 2015) and more likely to shift into new roles between years three and eight (Quartz et al. 2008).

The combination of social expectations and a feminized profession make a difficult combination for male teachers in particular. Although men are expected by society to serve as the primary breadwinners, they are often working in a profession that reflects the status, schedule, and salary expectations of a secondary wage earner. While the salaries of male teachers do not differ from those of female teachers, they may perceive their salaries as lower because of the social expectations placed upon them.

Moreover, as Andrew discovered, it is virtually impossible to support a middle-class lifestyle for a family of four on a teacher's salary in a major U.S. city. For those families who do choose a traditional route in which the father works and the mother stays home with the children (such families are in the minority in the United States now), teaching is essentially an unattainable career for the primary wage earner. Thus, we find that the influence of salary on career direction is mediated by teachers' gender and familial expectations.

Cultural Mediation

Salary is also mediated by culture. Although each culture has its own set of norms and expectations, Alicia specifically refers to her parents' "Asian culture" as an influence on her decision to become a teacher. Park (2009) discusses the challenges female teachers face in a traditional, patriarchal East Asian culture, which expects women to prioritize their husband's careers over their own and to emphasize child-rearing and homemaking. Alicia's choice to enter teacher preparation as a college freshman was influenced by a similar set of cultural norms, in which her parents encouraged her to select a profession that was "respectable," again reflecting expectations of teachers (Rury 1989), and that would be suited to future family obligations.

Park (2015) further discusses the process of identity renegotiation within new cultural contexts, arguing that experiences of privilege and marginalization are culturally relative and may intersect in varying ways. Here again, Alicia's life history reflects the same process of identity renegotiation. While she was growing up and living in her parents' home, Alicia was willing to go along with their view of an appropriate profession for a woman. However, over time as she gained independence, Alicia engaged in a process of identity renegotiation, evaluating her daily work life and current salary against what she saw among her peers.

This identity-making process ultimately led Alicia to establish her own views about the relationship between gender, culture, and work. In the end, Alicia found herself wanting more financial independence, willing to take more professional risks, and desiring more day-to-day autonomy in her work. For someone in a different cultural context, a teaching salary may have been sufficient. But for Alicia, reevaluating her salary through the lens of a renegotiated identity, she found her salary too modest to meet her needs.

Teaching Salaries in Context

As we observed in previous chapters, external, societal expectations and norms influenced teachers' perceptions of their work life and interpersonal interactions; here again in this chapter we find external, societal influences at play.

Teachers perceive their salaries through gendered and cultural lenses. Where one teacher may find the salary to be sufficient, another teacher in a different gender or cultural context may find the same salary lacking. Personal views about the role of men and women in the family, in relation to wage earning and childcare, influence teachers' perceptions of whether a salary is adequate to meet their needs, and changing models of the family, both within an individual and larger society, can affect these notions.

Thus, we see again that teacher career development cannot be understood in isolation. While there are certainly factors inside the classroom that influence teachers in their career decision making, teachers are continually weighing these factors against outside alternatives. In the case of salary, teachers evaluate appropriate compensation for their work against financial needs and professional options. Hanushek (2007), among others, has advocated for a differentiated pay scale based on effectiveness and ability to fill shortage areas. However, these are only two of the factors teachers consider in evaluating their salaries; cultural and gendered norms and expectations also serve as important lenses for interpreting salary and determining financial satisfaction with teaching.

Recommendations

Prioritize Salary

Our primary recommendation is to prioritize salaries in school budgets to the full extent possible. Although research on teacher career development shows that salary is one of many factors influencing recruitment and retention in the field, it is clear that low salaries do drive teachers from the classroom. In particular, districts should consider not only starting salaries but maximum district salaries as well as teachers' families grow and their financial needs in terms of housing, childcare, and education likewise increase. Imazeki (2002) has found that higher starting and maximum salaries can reduce teacher exits for both men and women in urban schools.

Furthermore, many school districts evaluate teacher salaries in relation to surrounding districts. This may be too limited a view. While higher relative salaries may pull teachers from surrounding districts, they have less impact on attrition decisions from the profession overall (Imazeki 2002). In today's work context, in which women and minorities have far greater opportunities compared with previous generations, teachers are not limited to classroom work (Bacolod 2007a). Instead, they are prepared to take on a wide variety of professional roles. Teachers' salaries should reflect a meaningful investment in human capital, one that values teachers' contributions and takes into account their efforts both inside and outside the classroom. These salaries should not reflect a semiprofession (Hoyle 2001) but a fully professional career in teaching (A. Hargreaves and Fullan 2012) that can be competitive with positions outside the field of education.

One school that has taken teacher salaries seriously is a charter school in the Washington Heights neighborhood of New York called The Equity Project (TEP). (http://www.tepcharter.org/). Serving a population in which over 90 percent of students are from low-income households, TEP recruits master teachers who earn a salary of $125,000 annually, plus the possibility of a $25,000 bonus. TEP does not fundraise or seek outside support for this salary structure. Instead, the TEP budget reflects a view of teachers as professionals who continually learn and grow together.

According to its website, TEP secures budget savings by putting teachers in roles of instructional leadership, professional development, whole-school processes coordination, and student activities leadership. In doing so, TEP is able to restructure the school budget to prioritize competitive salaries for teachers. Using this model, TEP has been successful in raising academic performance and "closing the Latino-white achievement gap." While TEP's exact approach may need modifications as it is scaled up, it can nevertheless serve as a model for schools seeking to increase their investment in teachers.

Invest in Identity

Given that decisions about salary are mediated by identity, we also strongly recommend that schools support diverse teacher identities. Currently, the teacher workforce is overwhelmingly white, female, and monolingual (Papay 2007). Not only does this fail to reflect the growing diversity in the U.S. student body, but it also provides a limited cohort of teachers from nonmajority backgrounds, including men and individuals from underrepresented racial, ethnic, and/or linguistic groups.

Without colleagues who look like them and share some of the same experiences, teachers lack a vital source of professional support. Previous research on racial identity development indicates the fundamental importance of having a peer group from the same background, who share similar gendered, racial, and other societal experiences, particularly when marginalized (e.g., Tatum 2017). Moreover, in the absence of a critical mass of teachers from a variety of backgrounds, teaching as a field may remain feminized, and teaching salaries may continue to be targeted toward female, secondary wage earners. Increasing the diversity of the teacher workforce may serve to strengthen it from the inside, while also raising its perceived status from the outside.

A promising model for investing in identity comes from outside teaching in the world of higher education. The Posse Foundation (https://www

.possefoundation.org/) aims to increase access for underrepresented groups in higher education by identifying academically talented high school students and placing them in "supportive, multicultural teams" of ten students at highly selective colleges and universities (Posse Foundation 2014). Selected students are provided with four-year, full-tuition scholarships as well as mentorship and leadership development. The underlying rationale behind Posse is that students benefit from higher education when they have a strong support network from like-minded individuals. The Posse Foundation has been highly successful, with 90 percent of scholars remaining in higher education through graduation and increasing the inclusiveness of campus cultures.

Although it operates in a different sector, The Posse Foundation can nevertheless provide a model for investing in teacher identity as well. Their underlying principle that a critical mass of individuals is needed to promote inclusion and leadership can be applied to the teacher workforce. By developing a stronger network of support among male teachers as well as teachers from underrepresented racial, ethnic, and linguistic groups, teachers may come to more strongly identify with teaching, rather than professional alternatives outside the classroom. And those who are outside of education may adapt their view of the profession, possibly leading to more professional salaries that meet the needs of a diverse group of wage earners.

Reflective Questions for Administrators

- Do teacher salaries reflect true professional commitment or semiprofessional work?
- What does my budget prioritize, and what values does it reflect? Can I restructure the budget to value the work of teachers more highly? If I do not have the autonomy to do so, can I advocate for teachers with the central office?
- Do both the starting and maximum salaries reflect the financial needs of the teachers?
- How do teachers' salaries compare with those in other districts and other sectors?

Reflective Questions for Teacher Educators

- In what ways am I promoting the teaching profession among a diverse group of prospective educators, including men and individuals from diverse racial, ethnic, and linguistic backgrounds?
- Do I promote a network of support and a sense of inclusion for all future teachers?
- How can I help future teachers navigate the interaction of their identit(ies) and their salary needs, both now and into the future?

Suggested Readings for Administrators and Teacher Educators

Goldstein, Dana. *The Teacher Wars: A History of America's Most Embattled Profession*. New York: Anchor, 2014.

In this book, Goldstein chronicles the history of the teaching profession from early America through today. She notes the importance of this subject because of the controversial nature of teaching, the integration of personal and professional in teaching, and the strong passion but lack of satisfaction among many teachers. By highlighting changing demographics, the feminization of teaching, and numerous reform efforts, Goldstein demonstrates how the salaries and conditions of teaching came to reflect their current structure. She also includes a thoughtful epilogue with practical suggestions for improving teaching, incorporating important points about teacher starting and maximum salaries, as well as the need to recruit both men and people of color into the profession. In this way, *The Teacher Wars* puts today's teaching salaries and teacher workforce into a historical context and argues for their reevaluation for a contemporary world.

Darling-Hammond, Linda. *The Flat World and Education: How America's Commitment to Equity Will Determine Our Future*. New York: Teachers College Press, 2015.

Like Goldstein's work, Darling-Hammond's book also puts the teaching profession into a larger, international context. Here she argues that globalization has resulted in a "flat world," one in which U.S. schools no longer operate alone but must instead compete with schools from around the world. Darling-Hammond argues that lingering inequalities in the educational system, including inequalities with respect to school funding, prevent U.S. schools from effectively competing internationally—to the detriment of all U.S. students. She demonstrates that a key investment in teacher quality, through both salaries and teacher education infrastructure, would be to the benefit of all. She illustrates the central importance of valuing teachers as professionals, both in culture and remuneration, in building for the future.

7

I Just Feel So Guilty

● ●

The Role of
Emotions in Leaving

Teaching is a profession of constant personal interaction. The center of this interaction is emotion (A. Hargreaves 1998; Jo 2014; Nias 1996; Yin and Lee 2012), and emotions are ubiquitous to the teaching experience (Trigwell 2012). A. Hargreaves (1998) argues that emotional teachers make some of the best teachers: "Good teachers are not just well-oiled machines. They are emotional, passionate beings who connect with their students and fill their work and their classes with pleasure, creativity, challenge, and joy" (835).

But teaching is not only emotional; it is also an emotional labor. Hochschild's (2012) theoretical construct of emotional labor suggests there are some professions in which individuals have to create or suppress certain feelings. Teaching is a profession in which teachers use their emotions as part of their professional work, but they also need to hide or produce emotions according to the expectations of others, in this case, students, administrators, colleagues, and parents. There are three characteristics of an occupation that requires emotional labor: "First, [the job] require[s] face-to-face or voice-to-voice contact with the public. Second, they require the worker to produce an emotional state in another person—gratitude or fear for example. Third, they allow the employer, through training and supervision, to exercise a degree of control over the emotional activities of employees" (Hochschild 2012, 147). Hochschild explains that not all professions that require emotional labor contain all these characteristics, but we argue that the teaching profession contains all of the above. Teachers are expected to interact face-to-face with students and administration, while interacting with parents and students voice-to-voice (in this case, either through the telephone, email, or social media) outside of school hours. Moreover, teachers are expected to manage their classrooms and the overall classroom experience with the production of emotions. Common emotions like respect, appreciation, care, and sometimes fear are often employed to manage students. Lastly, school officials and administrators closely monitor teachers' use of their emotions, or as it is often referred to in the profession—their dispositions. There is a level of surface acting (Hochschild 2012) that occurs as teachers are required to mask their true emotions. The expression of negative emotions (e.g., yelling, screaming, or crying) is simply not considered acceptable in the teaching profession.

Over the years, various studies have looked at the application of emotional labor within the field of education (Mawhinney 2008a, 2008b; Brennan 2006; Keogh et al. 2010; Yin and Lee 2012). Schutz and Lee (2014) discuss how emotional labor is connected and almost intertwined with teacher identity. Instruments like the Teacher Emotional Labor Scale (TELS), which is used on high school teachers, have shown that surface acting (Hochschild 2012) relates to emotional exhaustion (Çukur 2009). More recently, Acheson, Taylor, and Luna (2016) studied five foreign language teachers and what they term "the downward spiral of burnout." They found that while several variables contribute to burnout (e.g., "disproportionate burden for motivation, unsustainable emotional labor, emotional exhaustion, lack of self-efficacy, [more] emotional exhaustion, and job burnout" (532), the most prominent one is unsustainable emotional labor.

Persistent emotional labor can make for a destructive situation. Some researchers argue that the lack of teacher retention is attributed to the highly emotional nature of the work (Schutz and Lee, 2014; Schutz and Zembylas 2009). The most dangerous of these emotions is guilt.

The Emotional Labor of Guilt

Almost twenty years ago, A. Hargreaves (1994, 1998) argued that guilt is an emotion expressed in teaching, and it is part of the emotional labor (Hochschild 2012) expected within the profession. Guilt is a factor embedded into teaching on an international scale. Macmillan and Meyer (2006), in their research around Canadian special education teachers, found that teachers express guilt over an inability to reach perceived excellence in teaching. Farouk (2012) worked with English primary teachers, and van Veen and colleagues (2005) conducted research with one teacher from the Netherlands and examined his adaptations to reform. Both studies found that guilt resulted from a sense of not living up to expectations. Lamb (1983) mentions that the emotion of guilt itself, whether it comes from a rational or irrational place, will continue to make demands on the guilty party. Moreover, "We can only feel guilty about our *actions* (provided that we take them to be our actions), our *intentions to act*, and what we *take to be* our actions" (Lamb, 1983, 340). It is almost as if guilt is a common, almost expected, emotion for teachers to grapple with, one that can lead to consequences such as burnout and attrition.

A. Hargreaves (1998) explained how guilt can burn out teachers, and this dynamic has not changed over the decades, particularly in today's high-accountability context. He explains: "Overpersonalizing and overmoralizing about the emotional commitments of teachers without due regard for the contexts in which teachers work will only add to the intolerable guilt and burnout that many members of the teaching force already experience" (836). When discussing his research on active teachers, A. Hargreaves (1994) explains that there are two forms of guilt found in teaching: guilt traps and guilt trips: "Guilt traps are the social and motivational patterns which delineate and determine teacher guilt; patterns which impel many teachers towards and imprison them with emotional states which can be both personally unrewarding and professionally unproductive. Guilt trips are the different strategies that teachers adopt to deal with, deny, or repair this guilt" (142). Issues of burnout and leaving the profession fall under guilt traps. The guilt traps themselves, according to A. Hargreaves, are an intersection of four components of teachers' work: "the commitment to goals of care and nurturance, the open-ended nature of the job, the pressures of accountability and intensification, and the persona of perfectionism" (145).

This concept of guilt still resounds for teacher leavers—even years after leaving the profession. Jennifer was actually a teacher leaver twice. The first time she left, she recalled, "It was like remorse almost, like, 'Oh, my God, why did I leave? [Jennifer], you set as your purpose that you wanted to do science differently. You wanted to give Black and brown kids opportunities to see Black people doing science, and you left them.'" Eventually, Jennifer returned to the classroom, but several years later she made the decision to leave a second time: "Now, the emotions the second time, I felt guilt, because I left in the middle of the year, and I left a very vulnerable population, because in [the school], there were very few Black and brown kids. And I knew in [the school], I was one of only two non-gym, non-special ed. Black teachers, so I felt really guilty. . . . I thought to myself, 'Holy smokes. [Jennifer], you're leaving these kids,' and so there was a lot of guilt with that." Both times, Jennifer battled, and she still continues to wrestle with her guilt over leaving her students. She understood the importance of her role as a Black educator, as a symbol of the possible for Black and brown children to see themselves in the sciences.

Sasha, also a teacher of color, talked about how leaving was like a betrayal of sorts: "I think I felt like I betrayed something. I felt a little guilty 'cause it was like people need good teachers, and I could be a good teacher, and I felt like I really wanted to serve students who weren't being served. So I felt really guilty about that." But Sasha, and many others in our study, realized that they could still apply their mission-driven perspectives on teaching and advocacy in alternative ways. Sasha explained: "I also felt like I guess over time I came to understand that I could have a different role and that being a teacher is one role, and it's a very important role, but maybe if I was so frustrated with the school context and my life was going to be so difficult because of that, then it would be hard to stay in that role and not really healthy to do that. Not healthy for anybody." After leaving the classroom, Sasha managed to turn this guilt into advocacy work. She continues to stand on the frontlines, protesting for urban teacher and youth rights.

This chapter will highlight the holistic perspective through the stories of two participants: Lily and Lora. Specifically, the chapter captures the emotional aftermath of leaving teaching around two themes: (1) recognition of guilt; and (2) continued advocacy for their students. We found that teacher leavers continue to struggle emotionally with their choice to leave the classroom, but remain committed to affecting change in the educational system.

Lily

Career Overview. Lily's interest in education fueled her decision to dual major in educational studies and public policy as an undergraduate. Her interests lay in educational policy work, but she wanted to gain experience in teaching before moving into the policy realm. As Lily explained it, "I had a typical alternative-certification, out-of-college mindset where I was like, 'I'm not gonna teach for that long. It's just gonna be something I do to gain some experience before I do policy.'" Lily decided to enter teaching through a Teaching Fellows program with this mission in mind. The Teaching Fellows program requires participants to sign a two-year contract. During that two-year term, participants earn their master's degree in teaching while simultaneously teaching full time, receiving both a salary and graduate tuition remission.

Lily worked in a fifth- through eighth-grade middle school, teaching special education and language arts. She recalled that the first time she walked into her classroom was a memorable one: "I always remember walking into my classroom when I first got it, and it was empty. There was a hole in the wall. You could see through the wall to the outside. I mean, just stuff that would be covered with duct tape. I covered it with a poster." Like many teachers in under-resourced schools, Lily found herself with no textbooks, classroom management issues, and constant district reforms. But despite all of this, Lily really loved teaching, and she developed a strong rapport with the students. She explained, "After my second year, I decided that I really loved teaching and I was gonna stay for the long haul. I was happy there. I love the school." Thus, Lily changed her "typical alternative-certification, out-of-college mindset" and continued teaching in the school district.

During Lily's sixth year of teaching, the workload started to become too much. Lily reflected, "Some Saturdays I would be writing IEP's and crying at the same time because I was so stressed about getting everything done. . . . I shouldn't be doing all this work right now. This isn't one person's job. This is three person's job." The continued stress of the workload and the compromise of Lily's personal life made her question if she could really be a teacher "forever" toward the end of her sixth year. Lily decided to apply to a PhD program because "it was always in the back of my head. I think going into that [PhD program] I thought that I would return back to my educational policy roots. So I applied." Lily was accepted to the program and left her middle school classroom after six years of service.

Recognizing the Guilt. By the time of Lily's interview, she had already been out of the classroom for two years; yet she still continued to struggle with her decision to leave. She still had a strong identification with the school and continues to go back to the school regularly to work with the teachers. But this strong identity with the school carried with it a mass of emotions for Lily around her decision to leave. She started processing her emotions during a dialogue around her recent scholarly studies: "I've been reading a lot on teacher demoralization, and when I look back on myself, I think that I was feeling pretty demoralized because I couldn't do my job. I couldn't do really the right thing for my students."

Lily discussed the difficulty of mastering all her students' various learning abilities while also keeping them engaged in their learning. She found this to be an almost insurmountable task, as the only adult in the classroom: "I just felt like no matter what I did, everyone was not getting what they should have gotten, including myself, because I wasn't able to take care of myself personally sometimes because I was just trying to get my work done. I think that had that not happened to me and had I not had those feelings, I wouldn't have pursued the PhD. I think I would have stayed in teaching longer. . . . But I do think it [PhD program] was the right move, and I'm really glad that I did it, even though I have the feelings of guilt for leaving when I talk about it." This mention of guilt around leaving continually came up during Lily's interview. It was strong at times, as Lily even questioned if she had undermined her own principles by leaving. She explained, "I constantly feel like maybe I sold out a little bit and I should still be teaching, 'cause I can do it. . . . I don't know—and that maybe I should get back in there and do it."

Lily's guilty emotions around leaving the classroom seemed to be a constant tug on her. She even explained that the emotional part of leaving was the biggest continuing challenge she faced in leaving the classroom. Even though Lily had settled into a new career and was two years removed from the classroom, she still struggled with her decision: "I definitely always feel like maybe I should have stayed in teaching, but I feel I guess guilty for leaving. I think that's my greatest challenge. But I think that I'll get over that if I can—once I have a job and once I think that I am making a difference now with some of the things I'm doing. I think that all adds up, I'll get over that." Lily continued to harbor the idea that teachers on the front lines make more of a difference than those in higher education. She struggled to reconcile that difference during the interview itself. Ironically, Lily felt that if she went back to teaching today, she would be more prepared: "I think that if I went back to teaching, I would be an even better teacher because I'm aware of so much more, and I think that whatever flame was inside of me for social justice in terms of education, it's grown so much bigger."

Continued Advocacy. The flame of social justice is part and parcel of why Lily decided to leave. She wanted to use her doctorate to become an advocate for students within educational policy. Lily thought that with a PhD, she would be able to have more of an impact on urban students: "The whole reason I went into it [PhD program] is because I wanted to make an even bigger difference. I don't know now if I want to be a professor. Maybe I want to use my PhD to work for a nonprofit or to work for a school district, something where I can be more involved in what happens to students and teachers, 'cause my interests definitely lie in teaching and learning." Lily understood graduate school as a way of gaining a stronger voice. "I've become a lot more assertive, I think. When I was a teacher, I definitely always did what was asked of me, and I definitely—I don't think I spoke up a lot . . . now I've acquired that skill. . . . So I think that will help me if I want to have a higher-up position in a school district or in a nonprofit. I think that I'm better at speaking my mind."

Lily's notion of advocacy was already put to use serving the larger urban school district. She partnered with her neighbor to build a "friends of our local public school association." The purpose of was to encourage families to send their children to the local, urban school in her neighborhood and to discourage "white flight" from the community: "We're working on keeping local parents in the school and having them actually consider that [local, urban] school as an option, because so many people are just like, 'Well, as soon my kid is four, I move because I can't send them to a public school.' And they don't even know that we have this little gem right down the street from us." The association also developed outreach to the teachers in the local school. Aside from working with the parents, Lily also created partnerships with the teachers to help provide them with the supports they needed: "I'm working with supporting teachers, so I get to go into schools and support new teachers, which I love because I could have used more support as a new teacher. I like being able to give that to them and tell them that they're doing a good job instead of the opposite, which I think is what new teachers get a lot. So I'm just getting all these opportunities to explore my interests." In a way, Lily's support of teachers came full circle. She experienced demoralization as a teacher, but now she works actively to provide those supports that she herself missed by advocating on behalf of the parents, students, and teachers of her community.

Lora

Career Overview. Like the majority of the participants in our study, Lora did not enter college interested in becoming a teacher. During her undergraduate years, Lora studied psychology with a minor in Japanese. She explained how she was so focused on her studies that she neglected to think about the next steps of her life until the last semester of her senior year. It was during this semester that a Teach for America recruiter approached Lora, based on a peer recommendation, that she might be interested in the program. She went to an information session, where the recruiter really sold Lora on the idea of teaching: "It was the whole portraying of Black and brown kids not having access to a college education. . . . I didn't know that the statistics about certain populations being underachieving and many grade levels behind. . . . So as soon as I heard those statistics, those numbers, and sort of heard just pulling on the emotional strings, I was like 'Oh yeah. This is my mission. I want to do this.'" Reflecting on the situation, Lora recognized, "I do admit I had this sort of like hero mentality in some sense, more so it was like I really just wanted to do something that provided empowerment." Lora explained how Teach for America really framed this idea of "the hero savior situation," but Lora was hooked and wanted to give this a try, so she submitted her application.

Teach for America accepted Lora's application, and she ended up moving from the West Coast to the East Coast in order to teach. Lora taught middle school language arts for six years in a large, urban school district. She remembers her first year, which was similar to Lily's experience, with the challenges of classroom management, constant school reform, and lack of resources. "It was a tough first year, and eye-opening . . . to be in that environment, to be like wow, there's mice and there's chipped paint on walls, and why is it like this? So I had just a mix of emotions, just sadness, anger, frustration, stress, and how do I address all of this?" Lora also dealt with culture shock and adjustment coming from the West Coast to the East Coast and how that played itself out in the relationships with students.

Lora stayed at the school for three years before yearning for an experience to grow her teaching. She went to Japan to teach for a year and then came back to the district for another two years before deciding to leave. Lora entered teaching with a mission for social justice for Black and brown children. Six years later, Lora's decision to finally leave teaching was for the same mission: "I just felt like I was in a really oppressive environment and I was enabling this machine that I wanted to destroy. I didn't feel like I could kill it from within, I had to kill it from outside. So I thought, okay, I don't really feel like I have much voice here to do what I want to do, I feel like I need to do." Like Lily, Lora actually entered a PhD program in order to create educational change from the outside. Yet, the feelings of guilt around this decision nevertheless came through in her life history narrative.

Recognizing the Guilt. Lora talked at great length about her feelings and why she felt guilty for leaving teaching. She described a situation where she had a lively and animated discussion with her students. The volume was loud, but the students were participating in the class. Then the administrator came flying into the room, red faced and screaming at the students and Lora simultaneously for the loud volume. Lora recalled the experience with the students: "We were all sort of just lost, kind of felt demeaned, and it was a horrible feeling. I just couldn't take it anymore, and I felt guilty afterwards because I felt like I didn't want to be in that environment, but I left my kids in that environment."

Lora's interaction with the administration also fueled these emotions of guilt. When Lora told the principal that she was accepted into graduate school, the principal's response was, "You know what you should do? You should stand in front of your class and tell them why you are deserting them." Although Lora's immediate reaction was, "Really?!? Oh, okay, because I thought I would tell them that this is what you need to be doing too. You need to be seeking opportunities, you know, and bettering yourself." Reflecting back four years after leaving the classroom, she still internally struggles with the decision to leave: "I left because I want to make a bigger impact, what I think is a very common response for people who were in the classroom. What's the greater impact you can have than the one-on-one in the classroom, right? Like, and now you're just talking about it, you're just talking about them [students] as opposed to being there. It's just this weird space, but definitely guilt, like you deserted your kids, you know." Her principal's words continued to echo in her head, years later.

Continued Advocacy. Four years removed from teaching has not stopped Lora on her mission for advocacy for social justice. This concept of support for Black and brown children continually came out in her philosophy: "It's [large, urban school districts] this monster, to me. Now, I don't want to use that to say there's not great things happening, because at the end of the day, there's so many educators out there doing fantastic, amazing things in their classroom, but I don't mean to say that there's not great educators and schools and classrooms, but just the machine. It's frustrating that we can't figure out, or that people turn a blind eye to the fact that everyone doesn't have not even just equal, just like sufficient, like adequate opportunities." Although Lora was actively working toward her goal of a PhD, she continued to tutor students one-on-one in order to help them achieve the hurdles set in front of them by the urban school district.

As Lora was finishing her degree, she still questioned if the degree would help her debunk "the machine" of the school system. "I still don't know, what the hell do I do about that? Does having this degree gonna help me to do that? So just trying to find my own strategy to do that." While searching for her own strategy, Lora summarized her concepts of advocacy for urban students and teachers. Specifically, she mentioned the closing of twenty-four schools in the urban district at the time of the interview (all the schools closed were majority Black and Latinx schools). "I feel like society just accepts the fact that it's okay for certain folk to not have anything, and we sort of determine which kids deserve opportunities and which kids don't. You know, closing the schools, blindly, like without really even regard for who that's affecting and that's frustrating to me. It's just that, in particular, I feel like in terms of again, Black and brown, kids, I just feel like they obviously get the short end of the stick. My frustration is it just continues on every day."

These findings offer two key insights into the experiences of teacher leavers. First, leaving teaching can be an emotionally painful process that weighs on teachers for years after the decision is made. And, while that emotion is painful, it also drives future actions, often on behalf of students, schools, and communities.

The Emotional Labor of Guilt Revisited

The lives of these twenty-five teachers highlight the understudied component of how emotional guilt, and its complexities, continues years after teachers left the classroom. All teachers experienced a range of conflicting emotions, including guilt, upon leaving the profession, and they continued to struggle with these emotions years later. Lily and Lora are not alone in feeling "guilty" or feeling they were "selling out" on their students, as this was a theme we found consistently with our participants. Twenty-eight percent of the participants explicitly shared their guilt about leaving the classroom.

Both Lily and Lora felt the pressure of accountability and intensification within the school system—Lily with overworked expectations and Lora with the "oppressive machine" that was beating down on her and her students. The limited resources, the changing reforms, and the administrative pressures all seemed to play into the emotional labor of guilt. The care that both Lily and Lora displayed for their students seemed to be the biggest reason behind their continued guilt trip.

The guilt that Lily and Lora experienced generates a number of questions. Should they feel guilty for leaving their students? Since guilt is generated from emotional labor, is the guilt real or only perceived? Although these questions can bring forth various avenues of theoretical debate, at the end of the day, they both felt and experienced the emotion, whether it is expected in the profession or not. Lamb (1983) mentions that the emotion of guilt itself, whether it comes from a rational or irrational place, will continue to make demands on the guilty party. Moreover, "we can only feel guilty about our *actions* (provided that we take them to be our actions), our *intentions to act*, and what we *take to be* our actions" (Lamb 1983, 340). In essence, whether justified or not, the guilt was real for them. For Lily or Lora, and most of our participants, this guilt placed a demand on them to use that guilt as fuel for their advocacy agenda. They experienced the guilt for leaving the profession, but they were using the guilt to continue to care and provide for their students in a broader societal sense.

Macmillan and Meyer (2006) found when teachers cope with their guilt in positive ways, they are able to seek solutions from within or outside of policy. When they negatively cope with addressing guilt, there is often no resolution, no change, and the teachers are left feeling debilitated. It can be argued that Lily and Lora did not cope with their guilt in positive ways, which eventually ended their careers as teachers. But, we found that they currently use their guilt in positive ways to provide advocacy for students outside the classroom.

Guilt as Fuel for Advocacy

For Lily and Lora, their guilt came from the fact that they just could not cope with the system any longer. Lily revealed a further catalyst for her guilt—that she has become a better teacher but still chooses not to do the job. Lamb (1983) explains that guilt and shame can grow out of an inability to continue doing something or a choice to avoid it. For Lily, her ability to continue teaching can be viewed as a form of avoidance that continues to enhance her guilty conscience. While capacity and avoidance are salient in Lily and Lora's stories, they also demonstrate how guilt itself is the fuel for their continued advocacy.

Lily helped a local school by working with parents and teachers and continuing to live and work in the community. She may have left a classroom, but she remains an integral part of the urban school. Although Lora did not know what she wanted to do specifically with her degree, she has kept the agenda of supporting Black and brown students at the forefront of her mission to work with urban districts and teachers.

Lily and Lora are not unique in their continued advocacy for their urban students, school, and communities. The concept remains relevant for most of the participating teacher leavers. From our larger pool of participants, 60 percent of the teacher leavers continued in education or nonprofits in order to make a larger impact on schools and students. Amodio, Devine, and Harmon-Jones (2007) explain how "guilt implies a desire to repair one's transgression" (529). It is almost as if their emotional labor of guilt continues to thrive, even after leaving the profession, as their teacher identity remains embedded. Most are still working in education and teaching in some capacity in order to make "bigger change." We are not implying that guilt was the catalyst for continued educational advocacy for all our participants, but it certainly played a role for Lily and Lora, although not without causing some pain during the process.

These findings indicate important theoretical implications for understanding the career trajectory of teachers. While emotional labor has been seen as integral to the act of teaching, here we see that it remains relevant for years after leaving the profession. These teachers, who rarely discuss their emotional struggles with leaving teaching, came forward with powerful emotions during the life history interviews. The emotions continue under the surface as teachers and teacher leavers shape their ongoing careers as student advocates.

Recommendations

Lily and Lora provide a holistic look into the storied experience of former teachers and their experiences demonstrate the need for more emotional support for teachers while in the classroom and as they transition into new careers. The guilt traps (A. Hargreaves, 1994) that Lily and Lora experienced are ones we heard consistently throughout the interviews. We argue that there are various means administrators and school officials can use to lessen guilt traps and provide an emotionally healthy context for teachers. These strategies may also be applied to the teacher preparation context.

Resiliency and Teacher Care

Drawing on Day and Gu's (2009) work, which focused on three hundred veteran teachers in the United Kingdom, we emphasize the importance of school administration fostering a context of care. Day and Gu describe how seasoned teachers had a renewed sense of motivation and commitment to their work when there was "sympathetic and supportive management" (Day and Gu 2009, 454) built around a sense of professional trust. When teachers connect identity, commitment, and perceived self-efficacy, they become more resilient and offer a greater "reservoir of care" for their students (Day and Gu 2013). Sustaining teachers' "commitment, resilience, and effectiveness in the profession is a quality retention issue and that provision of appropriate in-school support is key to securing the professional quality of veteran teachers" (Day and Gu 2009, 454). When school administration supports teachers in achieving their goals, they also foster a resilience that can counter the emotion of guilt.

Likewise, there are many variables inside and outside a school that can lead to the development of guilt traps. For example, the constant pressure of account-ability (one component of guilt traps) in U.S. schools is often a governmental force housed outside the school. While this is a complex issue, we offer here some small ideas that can help lessen the emotional load of teachers.

Just as a guilt trap revolves around teachers committed to goals of student care (another component of guilt traps), we argue that schools should have the same commitment for teachers. Care, in this sense, is all-inclusive, as the physical self helps the body cope with the emotional self. Thirty-minute stress-reduction practices can be offered to teachers right after school. Some examples include exercise classes, walking/running clubs, meditation times, knitting clubs, and the like. The idea is that by providing these events right after school and on school grounds, and at least twice a week, will make it easier for teachers to participate and to forge bonds that can be used for mutual support. In essence, teachers' participation in these activities will help them physically and emo-tionally, and in turn, make them stronger teachers.

Shut Down Mode

Because teacher care assists in diminishing two components of the guilt trap, the other two components (open-ended job and perfectionism) can also be reduced through "shut down mode." The advent of technology has brought many advances to the teaching profession, but it has also created an environ-ment that escalates perfectionism and the open-ended nature of the job, as teachers are continually accessible to administrators, parents, and students. This creates added stressors that can easily be assisted with the school's email server. We argue that schools should shut down their servers from 6 P.M. to 7 A.M. on weekdays and all day on weekends. There are a number of European countries and corporate institutions that are following this model to alleviate stress on their employees, and we feel this small, yet powerful, change is a movement that should be happening in the schools.

The implications for teacher care and shut down mode are very small, yet achievable for all schools—especially under-resourced schools. They are not cost intensive, and they can certainly help to alleviate the guilt traps with the hope of sustaining more teachers in the field.

Recognition

It is also important to recognize that some current teachers in schools could be experiencing the emotion of guilt. For example, Sidney switched from a middle school to a high school, where she taught for another three years before leaving the profession. Sidney talked about her emotions at the time she was teaching at the high school: "My first year at the high school I really felt like I abandoned the kids at [the middle school] in a big way. I had a lot of regret and kind of beat myself up about that, I think, too much." Sidney makes an important point that administrators should remember, as active teachers may be struggling with guilt from leaving their previous school, administration, students, and communities. It is important for administrators to recognize this emotion in their teaching staff, and taking the time to listen and be emotionally supportive if need be in those moments, is a small, yet powerful administrative approach.

In addition, structuring time during the school day when teachers can process their emotions without the demands of students or technology provides teachers with the much-needed opportunity to make sense of their work lives. Arranging for teachers to have common planning times and space to discuss their own career development with administrators is essential.

Reflective Questions for Administrators

- How can I emotionally support teachers who are new to the school?
- What are ways that I can ensure a smooth transition for teachers to the school?
- How can I structure the school day to provide teachers with space to discuss their emotions?
- In what ways can I ensure that teachers are setting and reaching their professional goals?

Reflective Questions for Teacher Educators

- What is the best way to emotionally prepare preservice teachers to enter into field placements?
- How can I emotionally support preservice teachers when they are transitioning out of a field placement?
- If my preservice teachers experience feelings of guilt after leaving a field placement, how can I support them in working through those emotions? Are there ways to help prevent emotions of guilt from occurring?

Suggested Readings for Administration and Teacher Educators

Hochschild, Arlie Russell. *The Managed Heart: Commercialization of Human Feeling.* Berkeley: University of California Press, 2012.

> Although this book does not deal with teaching, teachers, or education directly, it is the main foundation for understanding teacher emotions. This update of the original 1983 version presents the groundbreaking research that generated emotional labor theory. Based on the professions of flight attendants and bill collectors, it highlights the aspects of emotional labor. Administrators and teacher educators will be able to see the connections of the emotional labor theory to the emotional aspects of the teaching profession.

Schutz, Paul A., and Michalinos Zembylas. (Eds). *Advances in Teacher Emotion Research: The Impact on Teachers' Lives*. New York: Springer, 2009.

This edited book is a good choice for both administrators and teacher educators. The authors share empirical and theoretical research on the emotional lives of teachers. Since this book looks at teacher emotions through various topics (e.g., administration, stress, identity, etc.), it is a valuable resource for all.

Day, Christopher, and Qing Gu. *Resilient Teachers, Resilient Schools: Building and Sustaining Quality in Testing Times*. New York: Routledge, 2013.

This book captures work from England's VITAE study on teachers' lives and careers. It provides extensive research demonstrating the centrality of resilience in teachers' well-being. It also offers the message that teacher resilience can be fostered within supportive school contexts and can be learned by the teachers themselves. Day and Gu's treatment of resilience is both theoretical and applied in nature, offering implications of individuals as well as systems of schooling.

Part IV

Addressing Teacher Attrition

● ●

8

Closing the Revolving Door

• • • • • • • • • • • • • • • • • • • •

Teacher Leavers' Final Lesson for the Profession

In this book, we set out to give voice to teacher leavers, individuals who voluntarily chose to leave the profession prior to retirement, from across multiple regions of the United States. We also set out to understand the teachers' reasons for making a career change and draw lessons from their experiences for school administrators and teacher educators. We found there is no single factor leading to the high rates of teacher attrition across the country. Teachers individually design their careers around their passions and identities (Savickas 2012). They continually negotiate the push and pull of multiple factors, both within and outside the educational system (Scott, Stone, and Dinham 2001). And they respond to both structural as well as personal influences as they navigate their career paths. Although we highlighted the stories of individual teachers in each chapter, often their experiences cut across multiple areas as they crafted their professional paths.

Just as no single factor influenced these teachers' decisions to leave the profession, there was no "magic bullet" for keeping them engaged and sustained in the classroom. However, we did identify several steps that educational leaders can take to promote a professional climate in which teachers' work is valued and teachers as individuals are respected. In this final chapter, we offer perspectives and strategies that may validate the work of teaching and strengthen the profession over time. We provide specific recommendations to couple mission with professionalism, engagement with respite, and education with the larger workforce to transform a "revolving door" into a stable and committed teaching force.

Theme #1: From Mission-Driven Teaching to Mission-Guided Teaching

While conducting this research project, we were quite shocked as to how many of the teacher leavers became emotional, to the point of crying, during the life history interviews. Some teacher leavers who left the classroom over seven years ago were unexpectedly and highly emotional. This is unusual for a career change. We do not imagine that former accountants cry over missing their Excel spreadsheets, so why are former teachers so emotional all these years later? Certainly one aspect is that teacher leavers worked with people, not software, and they felt a loss over these interpersonal relationships. However, we found that there was an additional layer of loss causing these emotions—the loss of how they imagined a teaching career.

Santoro and Morehouse (2011) discuss this idea among their sample of teacher leavers, those they call "principled leavers." They define principled leavers as follows: "Akin to conscientious objectors who refuse to fight wars they deem unjust, principled leavers resign from teaching on grounds that they are being asked to engage in practices that they believe are antithetical to good teaching and harmful to students" (Santoro and Morehouse 2011, 2671).

In their research case, principled leavers taught for five years or more, expected to teach in "high-poverty" schools for the long term, and some major catalyst (i.e., standardized testing, scripted curriculums, etc.) caused a change of heart toward teaching, although it was not the sole reason for the decision to leave. Interestingly, participants who would be considered principled leavers in our study (see table 8.1) also turned out to be "shifters," according to Olsen and Anderson's (2007) definition. Their notion is that shifters stay committed to urban youth, but they do so as teacher educators, administrators, and other nonclassroom teachers within the field of education. In this way, shifters widen their influence and impact on urban youth, underserved communities, and fellow colleagues.

In this study, 48 percent of our teacher leavers can be categorized as principled leavers because, although there are complexities of variables that lead to the decision to exit, they explicitly left for moral reasons. For example, Lora left because "I was enabling this machine that wanted destroy, I didn't feel like I could kill it from within, I had to kill it from outside. So I thought, okay, I don't really feel like I have much voice in here [in the classroom] to do what I want to do, I feel like I need to be this like leader of urban ed, right, so I can be con-

Table 8.1
Principled Leavers/Shifters and Occupation

Participant	Principled leaver		Current job
	No	Yes	
Abigail		X	African dance school owner/ higher education
Alice	X		Business
Amber	X		Higher education
Andrew	X		Education administration
Anita		X	Community outreach education
Ayana		X	Community education administrator
Beatrice		X	Graduate school (education)
Catherine	X		Medicine
Erika	X		Graduate school (education)
Jennifer	X		Higher education
Jeremy		X	Higher education
Jordan	X		Technology
Kaitlin	X		Politics
Kelsey	X		Caregiver
Lily		X	Graduate school (education)
Liana		X	Educational policy and evaluation
Lora		X	Graduate school (education)
Mason	X		Pastor
Miles		X	Community education administrator/ graduate school (education)
Monica	X		Medicine
Nina	X		Medicine
Patricia	X		Graduate school (science)
Sasha		X	Higher education
Sidney		X	Program evaluation/graduate school (education)
Susan		X	Nonprofit

sidered this expert, have some credibility and do some things with the beast." Another example is Miles, who left after twenty-three years of teaching: "I was so angry, and so sad, at the district and I felt like this was an opportunity to do the reform that these central office people talk about all the time, especially the superintendent, and I was just so pissed. . . . I'd also seen a window into the toxicity and the dysfunction of central office. I'd been in the system for almost twenty-five years, and it's the same crap that we've been dealing with year after year."

In the case of the principled teacher leavers, like Lora and Miles, we found that every one of them remains connected to serving in urban communities in one form or another. This constitutes a shift within the profession to a context in which teachers can have greater impact. Although two of our principled leavers taught for less than five years (which was Santoro and Morehouse's criteria), they were both teachers of color who faced additional challenges because of their desire to be change agents and pursue a social justice mission (Lynn 2002; Mawhinney, Rinke, and Park 2012; Tolbert and Eichelberger 2016). All the principled leaver participants remain connected to urban education in some way. Some are doctoral candidates focused on urban education, others are directly serving the urban community, and still others are training the urban teachers of tomorrow.

What these principled teacher leavers all have in common is their commitment to teaching as a mission-driven profession. This image of the teacher hero is seen in film and often reinforced through an emphasis on social utility in teacher education programs (Bulman 2002, Watt et al. 2012). Yet we find that the mission-driven approach to teaching, which does show strength, heart, and commitment, can have detrimental effects on the teachers themselves. As we saw with our participating principled leavers, leaving was often associated with guilt and dissonance in the identity-construction process (Macmillan and Meyer 2006).

This brings to light a possible shortcoming in teacher education programs that adopt an activist disposition (Boggess 2010). What happens when teachers, who are trained as activists and change agents, are unable to enact the change they imagine in schools and with their students? They have been prepared to disrupt the status quo, but they may not be empowered to do so. This discrepancy calls for a reconsideration of this approach, and a move from mission-driven teaching to *mission-guided teaching*. In this case, mission-guided teaching and the professionalism of the career are not separated from each other; instead, they are coupled together.

International comparisons show that countries such as Finland, which regularly attains top student scores, place a significant emphasis on developing the professionalism of teachers through teacher education (National Conference of State Legislatures 2016). By emphasizing both advocacy as well as professionalism, teaching can become a profession *with* justice-oriented approaches instead of a profession *for* justice-oriented approaches. Ultimately, we need to exchange the image of the teacher hero with the image of a justice-oriented professional.

The Role of Mission in Lynnette's Practice

I have evolved in my thinking about the role of social justice in teacher education. I used to be a teacher educator who tried to build a mission-driven teacher identity for my undergraduate urban education majors—an identity I took on myself. While writing this book, I taught in a five-year urban education program that culminates in both bachelor's and master's degrees, coupled with an

ESL certification. During the preservice teachers' freshman year, they take a course with me called Introduction to Urban Education. It is here that my former colleague, Tabitha Dell'Angelo, and I really saw this course as laying the foundation for our social justice-focused urban teacher education program.

On the very first day of class, I used to stand in front of the preservice teachers and say, "I will make it very clear that I have an agenda. My goal at the end of this class is to make you into social justice foot-soldiers." After this class and five more years of developing mission-driven teachers, I have slowly seen the detrimental effects that build up in these teachers. This guilt is reflected in our students who have gone on to be teachers in the classroom, and in particular, among teachers who do not choose to teach in urban areas. For instance, I had dinner with a former student who was struggling with the fact her teaching job was in an affluent neighborhood. She and other students in similar settings saw themselves as "sell outs," even though they were working diligently each day to support their students' development.

My teaching has changed, as I better understand the impact a mission-driven approach has on the teachers themselves. I now see that a mission-driven framework can be detrimental to my preservice teachers' emotional well-being and can possibly shorten their time in the classroom. Through the life histories of these teacher leavers, I have come to understand that my approach to teacher education needed to shift drastically.

Part of this process started with my own reflection and shift concerning my identity as a teacher. I had to switch my own identify as a mission-driven teacher to a mission-guided teacher by spending some time in personal reflection. The first question I asked myself—How do I manage and balance a mission-guided approach to teaching?—came with the understanding how much I need to rely on my hobbies and "other identities" to not make teaching an unhealthy habit.

In my former Urban Education Seminar elective course, the preservice teachers have a two-week intensive experience completing eighty hours of field time in a classroom and conducting a service-learning project. Since I lived in the city of this course, I brought the preservice teachers to a Taekwon-do class. Taekwon-do has been a part of my life for over twenty years, and it is how I find fulfillment and balance in my new mission-guided teaching approach. The preservice teachers had fun experiencing the sport, but they also saw the importance of hobbies for balance (see recommendations in chapter 3) and having other identities. In this case, they got to see my other identity as a marital artist intimately. One of my former students has been an urban special education teacher for three years, and she even decided to take up Taekwon-do and has been using it as balance. This is not to say that all preservice teachers should be martial artists, but they should have some hobby that helps them to balance the stress of teaching.

The second question I had to ask myself is, What guilt do I still have from leaving the high school classroom? Like the principled leavers and teacher shifters in this research project, I also struggle with the guilt of "leaving my students behind." Although I was able to balance that because I was with some of my high school students at the university level with my first institution, I realized there was still some lingering guilt in my emotions. I think I unfairly emphasized the mission-driven teaching to my preservice teachers as a "mea culpa" for my own high school classroom exit. As I was able to let that go, the emphasis on a mission-guided teaching approach in my pedagogical practice with my preservice teachers was much more natural, fluid, and unforced.

Theme #2: From Burnout to Resilience

"You know, if I was able to have a sabbatical, I think I would still be teaching now." (Amber)

Amber's off-handed comment brings up a vitally important point about teachers' careers. Teaching is a profession that requires heavy emotional labor (Hochschild 2012), which is made all the more intense by an expectation that teachers also drive educational change. Service incentives for teachers might provide a respite from the labor, while also promoting intellectual growth in teachers' areas of interest. As Amber suggested, research shows that sabbaticals can be an easy and inexpensive solution that promotes teacher retention.

The word "sabbatical" literally comes from the word "Sabbath," meaning a time of rest. In an age where teachers have chronic stress that leads to departure from the profession, the simple solution could be to just grant a time of rest for teachers. In U.S. public schools, teachers used to be eligible for a sabbatical once every seven years, although this policy is no longer widespread. Sabbaticals are often given with either full pay or partial pay, with the expectation that continuous professional development (CPD) would occur during the time off. CPD might consist of attending graduate classes, workshops, relevant travel, or even internships that might provide new expertise the teachers could bring to their students. In short, sabbaticals allow teachers "a chance to learn from others as well as share expertise and build partnerships" (Kelley 2016, 26).

Moreover, sabbaticals are proven to provide the respite and rejuvenation that lead to a renewed commitment to the profession (Miller, Bai, and Newman 2012). Otto and Kroth (2011) explained there are multiple benefits to sabbatical. "Organizations use sabbatical leave to retain employees by preventing burnout which leads to low productivity, depressed morale and high turnover. They use it as a recruitment tool to draw in top performers" (Otto and Kroth 2011, 30). It is a simple service incentive that can be used for both teacher recruitment, and more importantly, for teacher retention.

Currently, many districts are cutting sabbaticals from their school budgets or at the negotiation tables with unions. Furthermore, many charter schools are nonunionized and do not have the right to ask for a sabbatical. Some teachers are simply unaware that sabbaticals are a part of their contract. The research shows that sabbaticals do not incur additional cost to the district (Downing et al. 2004) and in fact save money by reducing continuous, pricey, and time-consuming searches for teachers. The national cost for teacher turnover is estimated to be $7.34 billion (Carroll 2007). Barnes, Crowe, and Schaefer (2007) show how urban schools, like the Chicago Public Schools that lose $17,872 per teacher leaver, should implement retention programs that will ultimately save the district millions of dollars—sabbaticals are a cost-saving option for districts.

Sabbaticals are not a new concept and have been proven effective. In 1925, the Department of Interior reported on sabbaticals as incentives to teachers working within city school systems (Deffenbaugh 1925). They argued that sabbaticals gave teachers time to "study, travel, or the recovery of health" (Deffenbaugh 1925, 15). Sabbaticals were encouraged in Massachusetts' schools in the 1970s in order for "(1) personal refreshment and reassessment, (2) increased knowledge of subject matter, [and] (3) a broader perspective on education, the world, and your place in both" (Rossi 1973, 36), and they were even analyzed and found effective in three urban districts in 1980 (Moore and Hyde 1980).

There are various aspects of sabbaticals that can be reconsidered in order to maximize the benefit to teachers and urban schools. One change to consider is the timing of sabbaticals. The teacher leavers in this study averaged about seven years of teaching, which is already longer than the national average of five years in the classroom (Gray and Taie 2015; Ingersoll 2003). Most often sabbaticals are granted during year seven, which seems to be one year too long before the profession's burnout factor takes a permanent toll. Thus, districts should reconsider providing sabbaticals after the fifth year of teaching. This seems to be the optimal timing for teacher retention. As an example, New Zealand, known for an emphasis on work-life balance (HSBC 2016), provides sabbaticals for teachers after their fifth year of teaching (TeachNZ 2017), which seemed to be effective throughout the country. Another option to consider is varying lengths of sabbatical terms. Often, districts provide half-year or one-year sabbaticals, which should absolutely be maintained. But an alternative would be to offer a variety of short-term sabbaticals (Sklarz 1991) that can consist of two weeks, thirty days, or six weeks of CPD.

All of these benefits have been proven in a study of sabbaticals for teachers working in "challenging schools" in England (Downing et al. 2004). The design of this scheme (as they called it) for sabbaticals was based on Harland and Kinder's (1997) typology of outcomes for CPD. The outcomes are outlined in their model (see table 8.2) and can easily be used with other urban districts that are considering implementing sabbaticals.

Table 8.2
Harland and Kinder's (1997) Typology of CPD Outcomes, as Represented in Downing et al. (2004, 58)

Informational
This refers to the acquisition of professional facts or news. Unlike the development of increased skills and knowledge, it does not assume a deeper or critical understanding of the new material.

Material and provisionary
Physical resources acquired as a result of the sabbatical, including curriculum resources, equipment, and books.

New awareness
Defined as a perceptual or conceptual shift from previous assumptions. This may relate to perceptions of appropriate content and delivery of a specific curriculum area, or to more general expectations about pedagogical or management issues.

Affective changes
Positive emotional responses to the sabbatical experience, for example, as a result of involvement in the activities themselves, the development of new knowledge or practices, or the experience of spending time away from regular duties.

Motivational changes
Enhanced enthusiasm for their work or increased motivation to implement the results of a sabbatical experience.

Value congruence
This refers to the process of acceptance and internalization of a new set of values highlighted by the sabbatical experience.

Skills and knowledge
Developments in professional skills and knowledge.

Changes in practice
This includes changes in actual practice in any area, including teaching methods, developments to the curriculum and management systems.

Institutional
Outcomes relating to the development of other members of staff could encompass the full range of outcome types for the teacher. In addition, sabbatical activities may generate outcomes concerning wider whole-school issues, and these include development of school structures, ethos, management, and staffing as well as outcomes that might be viewed as more traditional school-level professional development.

The participating teachers on sabbatical lived in urban areas like London and Manchester with 130 teachers in total taking sabbatical (97 primary, 14 secondary, and 19 special needs schools) (Downing et al. 2004). The teachers took sabbaticals anywhere from a three-week block of time to six weeks total. Using the CPD typology of outcomes (Harland and Kinder 1997), a sample of the evaluators' (Downing et al. 2004, iii) findings concerning the teachers on sabbatical were:

- 87 percent experienced improvements in confidence, refreshment, and self-esteem
- 67 percent reported increased motivation
- 87 percent raised knowledge and skill level
- 83 percent reported changes in pedagogical practice
- 56 percent claimed that the sabbatical resulted in school-wide practice changes

Although this is just one sample of the numerous findings concerning sabbaticals, the most important insights came from a series of follow-up interviews conducted with teachers after their sabbaticals were completed. Thirty teachers out of the thirty-nine that participated in the follow-up interviews maintained their sense of confidence and motivation toward the profession.

A last option to consider is sabbatical funding. In the case of longer-term sabbaticals (i.e., half-year or full-year), the district often cuts the teachers' salaries, say by 25 percent, in order to pay for substitute teachers. For short-term sabbaticals (i.e., two-week to six-week), districts can set up what Rossi (1973) referred to as a "sabbatical bank." A sabbatical bank can consist of: (1) "interest-earning revolving fund for teacher payroll deductions and municipal treasuries" (Rossi 1973, 37) or (2) unused sick days applied toward the sabbatical term. Downing and colleagues (2004) also suggest that having a permanent "floating teacher" to fill in for the teachers on sabbaticals can help to maintain consistency throughout the school and the classrooms.

In short, there are a variety of approaches and changes to consider with sabbaticals (see table 8.3), as sabbaticals have been proven to be an active component to assisting teachers' mental health and ultimate retention in the field.

If we consider the importance of maintaining sabbaticals while also providing changes and various options to the service incentive, urban schools

Table 8.3
Comparison of Current and Needed Sabbatical Options

Sabbatical currently	Sabbatical changes needed
It is not a readily available option. If it is an option, it is not advertised well to teachers.	Make sabbatical more available, and use it as a service incentive to recruit teachers.
Available only as half-year or one-year leave	Continue with half-year and one-year leaves, but also add other options: two-week sabbatical, thirty-day sabbatical, etc.
Available after seven years of service	Available after five years of service
Reduction in salary to pay for substitute teachers	Continue reduction in salary as one option, but also consider alternative "sabbatical bank" financial options.

can ultimately achieve what Mulholland and colleagues (2017) discovered in Scotland: "In the long run, [sabbaticals] could impact positively on teacher wellbeing, their capacity to manage the content of work, and significantly, enhance the learning experiences and achievements of the young people they engage with across their teaching career." Using Downing and colleagues (2004) sabbatical examples, we dared to outline what could have been the alternative path for Amber (figure 8.1), if she were granted that sabbatical she wished for.

Theme #3: From Isolation to Connection

Together these insights suggest the need for a broader lens, one that looks beyond the work of the classroom to situate teaching within national and international settings as well as social, economic, and professional contexts. We can no longer view teacher attrition simply as individuals tiring of the demands of the classroom; we must instead view teacher attrition as a complex negotiation among multiple competing factors. Adopting this broader lens may promote a dynamic teaching profession for years to come.

In contrast, the field of education tends to operate in relative isolation. Teachers are frequently prepared within schools of education, rather than in a broader context, such as a school of liberal arts, sciences, or engineering. Although connections are made across campus departments, these contacts can be tenuous or even fraught due to disciplinary cultures and the silos of the university setting. Once teachers are hired into schools, by nature of their work, they spend most working days in the same building. Professional development that does occur is typically school- or district-based, paired with further formal education within a school of education. Rarely do funds allow classroom teachers to attend national or international conferences. While there are strengths to this model, such as a strong school-based community, an unintended consequence is the relative isolation of teachers within the world of education.

However, education actually has much in common with other human service fields, including social work, psychology, and nursing, among many others. Education is categorized as a semiprofession, where it shares characteristics such as a feminized workforce, moderate status and prestige, and an emphasis on relationship building with other similar occupations (Hargreaves 2009; Hoyle 2001). As one example, the national accreditation standards for programs in social work and programs in teacher education share many features: they both address competencies related to diversity, research-based practice, ethical conduct, and engagement with the larger community (Council on Social Work Education 2015; Council for the Accreditation of Educator Preparation 2013). Education also shares a similar retention rate with both nursing

Amber, a 14-year veteran English teacher, completed her Ed.D. in literacy while teaching full time. This was a catalyst, among other variables (boredom—"I could be teaching *Mice and Men* for the next 35 years of my life... I was already kind of bored") leading Amber out of the profession. The following figure displays what it would look like if Amber were granted a one-year sabbatical.

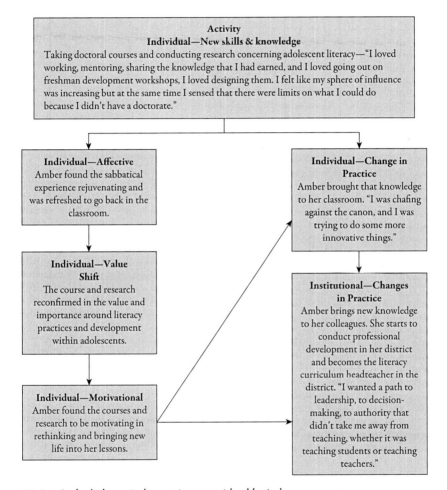

FIG. 8.1 Amber's theoretical career journey with sabbatical

and accounting (Keller 2007) as well as common mentoring practices with medicine and business (Ehrich, Hansford, and Tennent 2004).

Not only does education share much with other occupations, but research has also demonstrated that broader professional opportunities matter to teachers as they select and sustain their career paths. Johnson (2007) first introduced the notion of a hidden subsidy for education, an artificially inflated workforce resulting from limited opportunities for women and underrepresented groups in other fields. Bacolod (2007a) examined this hypothesis using data from 1960 to 1990 and showed that the existence of wider professional opportunities for women did in fact influence the number and quality of individuals entering teaching. Even within education, alternative opportunities matter. Murnane and Olsen (1990) demonstrated that those teachers with greater professional opportunities, based on their academic ability, spent fewer years in the classroom. As their duration increased with salary growth, Murnane and Olsen argued for differentiated salary scales by field and academic ability in response to these opportunity costs for teaching.

The field of education must take seriously the broader labor context in which it operates. It can no longer rely on a hidden subsidy to enhance the workforce; instead, education must actively compete with a range of fields to recruit and retain teachers. Undergraduate and graduate students have a variety of opportunities available to them. Even licensed teachers, such as those highlighted throughout this book, have demonstrated their willingness to pursue other career paths. Teaching needs to remain attractive by promoting working conditions that support both the intrinsic and extrinsic rewards of the profession, encouraging community, open communication, autonomy, and teacher care in a context of reliable stability, realistic workload, and competitive salary.

Reducing the Isolation of Teaching

Despite the relative isolation of teaching, there are many avenues available for broadening our perspective and learning from others. One possible lens, which has been mentioned at several points throughout this book, can be directed toward educational systems outside the United States. It has been widely publicized that test scores in the United States fall below those in many industrialized countries on the Program for International Assessment (PISA) exam (Ripley 2016, Dec 6), which measures students' academic performance in mathematics, science, and reading. As a result, a whole body of literature has emerged on the features of effective school systems around the world, those capable of either sustaining or increasing levels of student achievement. Darling-Hammond and Lieberman's (2012) volume *Teacher Education around the World* captures the key features of education in a number of countries and highlights that support for the profession and investment in the knowledge and skills of teachers are common features internationally. Sahlberg's (2010) *Finnish Lessons* likewise captures the rigorous selection and preparation that Finnish teachers undergo, along with their accompanying professional respect. These, among other works, offer a window into the most effective educational systems, with concrete lessons for recruitment, preparation, and support of teachers that can be applied to U.S. schools.

Another possible lens is to connect education more explicitly with related human service professions. We already know that there are many commonalities across these professions, including the relationship-centered nature of the work, status and prestige, and relevant competencies. Some of the explanatory concepts used throughout this book, such as burnout (Maslach, Schaufeli, and Leiter 2001) and emotional labor (Hochschild 1983), come not from the field of education but rather from psychology and sociology, respectively. Likewise, vocational psychology is a well-developed field in and of itself with theoretical concepts, applications, and strategies that are applicable to a wide range of fields (e.g., Lent, Brown, and Hackett 1994; Swanson and Gore 2000; Savickas 2012). Other research looks at the psychological and health effects of commitment, autonomy, relationships, and workload across multiple professions (e.g., Tham and Meagher 2009; Galletta, Portoghese, and Battistelli 2011; Plaisier et al. 2007; Budge, Carryer, and Wood 2003). Here again, understandings gathered from a wide range of fields are directly relevant to teaching, allowing education to draw from a deeper pool of ideas.

Finally, the benefits of teaching are often compared among sectors, such as between primary and secondary teaching, rural and urban teaching, or public and private teaching (e.g., NCES 2008). However, the extrinsic benefits of teaching are rarely compared across sectors. Some limited international research has examined the salaries of teachers in comparison to other fields, finding them lower than other fields in Latin America (Liang 2000) and declining in relative pay in Europe (OECD 2005). However, more direct comparisons, which include salary as well as workload, autonomy and control, and other professional features, would be valuable to prospective and practicing teachers, as well as administrators who wish to keep their schools competitive. Identifying a commonly agreed upon method for compensating teachers, which captures not only hours taught but also out-of-classroom efforts to support student growth, is also essential.

Overall, a number of promising educational innovations first emerged in other fields, such as the residency structure from medicine, which is now applied to teacher preparation (Berry, Montgomery, and Snyder 2008), and the case study method for analyzing pedagogy, distinctive to the field of business (Grossman 2005). Recently, the CAEP teacher education accrediting organization adopted the Plan-Do-Study-Act (PDSA) cycle (Council for the Accreditation of Educator Preparation 2015), which is a process that comes from the healthcare industry. Specifically, it means "testing a change by developing a plan to test the change (Plan), carrying out the test (Do), observing and learning from the consequences (Study), and determining what modifications should be made to the test (Act)" (Institute for Healthcare Improvement 2017, 1). The PDSA cycle, a feature of the process improvement literature, has been a recommended tool for continual quality improvement in teacher education.

Cross-fertilization of ideas can only benefit education and should be encouraged among practitioners, administrators, and teacher educators.

Interdisciplinary conferences that address cross-cutting themes and the support to both attend and collaborate with colleagues outside the field of education can move education into the broader intellectual and professional market. Although all methods introduced to education should be vetted to ensure they benefit students as well as teachers, there are nonetheless promising advances that can be introduced from outside the field.

How Carol Looks Outside the Teaching Bubble

When I chose to become a teacher leaver myself, it was not due to some specific source of dissatisfaction. Rather, I was seeking greater stimulation in what I did every day. I loved and still love working with students, but I also wanted to continue learning new skills, interacting with new people, and trying new things. While there is space for such experimentation within education, the possibilities are multiplied when we look across disciplines.

After completing graduate school within a traditional school of education, I sought out my first teaching position at an institution where I could interact with educators as well as learn from those outside the field. I ended up teaching at a liberal arts college, where education was one of many departments, rather than a separate school. Here, I taught a first year seminar to freshman from multiple disciplines as well as a course introducing historical, pedagogical, and policy themes in urban education to students from across campus, including future teachers as well as those generally curious about the field of education. I also learned a great deal about how to support service learning in the local community from my interactions with the campus-wide Center for Public Service.

Following this first position, I moved to my current institution, where the education department is housed within a School of Social and Behavioral Sciences and incorporates education, psychology, social work, sociology, and criminal justice. There are many such approaches to higher education organization, such as pairing education with health professions, communication, and other related fields. Within the School of Social and Behavioral Sciences, five faculty—myself, Daria Hanssen, Julie Raines, Janet Stivers, and Stacy Williams—have brought together a community to share commonalities and learn from each other.

An example of one such interdisciplinary initiative stemmed from the faculty's aspiration to construct more inclusive environments in our courses, particularly for students from underrepresented groups in higher education. When we sat down to discuss this effort, we also recognized that in each field—education, psychology, social work, and criminal justice—we sought to prepare future professionals to interact effectively in a diverse world. As a group, we decided to draw upon the strengths of each discipline to improve our collective practice, an effort we called *Creating an Inclusive Community*. We drew resources from each field to inform our discussion and shared strategies that would apply across specialties.

From education, we read *Waking Up White* (Irving 2014) and *Raising Race Questions* (Michael 2015) to better understand racial identity development. From the field of counseling psychology we read *Race Talk and the Conspiracy of Silence* (Sue 2016) to develop new strategies for talking about race in the college classroom. Daria Hanssen, a social work faculty member, introduced us to her statement of intent, based on the social workers' code of ethics (National Association of Social Workers 1996). She used it as a model for fostering respectful dialogue about difficult topics in her courses. Finally, Addrain Conyers, a criminal justice faculty member, shared his game of stratified monopoly (Fisher 2008), an experiential tool that demonstrates class stratification and its consequences for society. Through this process, we all gained new insights and strategies, which we applied in various ways to our own courses and also shared with an even wider group of faculty, staff, and administration across campus, further widening the sphere of learning.

Another example of cross-fertilization comes from my current Science, Technology, Engineering, and Mathematics (STEM) Methods for Elementary Teaching course. Finding that these teaching candidates were seeing little elementary science taught in grades 1–6 classrooms because of testing and other pressures, I tried to think outside of the box and reached out to the Mid-Hudson Children's Museum, adjacent to our campus, for field experiences. At first, our preservice teachers developed brochures to guide parents and caregivers through the academic and school readiness features of the various exhibits. However, through multiple visits to the museum, I observed the effective use of a science cart to encourage open-ended exploration of new concepts by visitors from a wide range of ages and ability levels.

Inspired by this concept, but wanting to encourage greater interdisciplinarity in mathematics and engineering, I proposed that our candidates develop Discovery Boxes, interactive tools to encourage children's exploration of interrelated science, math, and engineering concepts. Provided with feedback from the museum director and educator to make instructional resources accessible and bilingual, as well as hints for how to grab children's attention in this informal setting, our class set out to develop these Discovery Boxes. Here again I learned from my students as they used their creativity to construct visually attractive learning tools that encouraged the exploration of forces, life cycles, measurement, data, and more (see figure 8.2 for examples). The Discovery Boxes were then donated to the museum following the final assessment for use by visitors of all ages.

The Discovery Boxes represent a true collaboration, not nominal outreach from higher education to the local community, but rather a mutually beneficial and equitable partnership in which we both learned new approaches. The

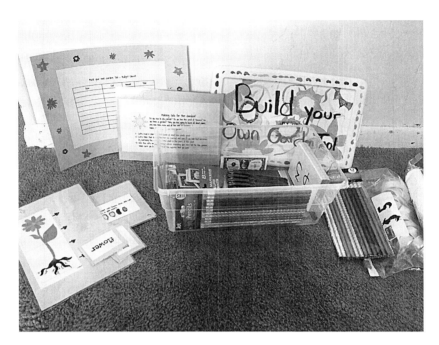

FIG. 8.2 Examples of candidates' created Discovery Boxes

expansion of such cross-fertilization of ideas and methods can serve to broaden the perspective of everyone involved and may promote resilience and longevity in the profession.

Final Thoughts

Through this research, we set out to capture the voices of a hidden group of teachers, those who had voluntarily left the classroom. We also intended to shed light on the reasons behind their departure and the resulting lessons for the profession. We found, as with many things in education, that we need to build on the existing strengths of the profession while continuing to grow. We found that maintaining the mission of teaching while infusing greater professionalism, nourishing engagement through opportunities to both rest and explore, and connecting teachers with related professionals can sustain educators in their careers over time.

Acknowledgments

Above all, we would like to thank all of our teacher participants. You so willingly shared your personal life stories with us, often sight-unseen. We were just voices, sometimes across the country, and you trusted us with your stories. We value all that you had to share, through the positive stories and tears, and we hope that we successfully represented your important stories to others. Thank you.

We would also like to thank our current and former institutions for the financial support that made this project possible. Specifically, we would like to thank The College of New Jersey's School of Education mini grant and Marist College's Office of Academic Affairs summer research grant for funding this effort. We would also like to thank The College of New Jersey for granting Lynnette a sabbatical in order to provide uninterrupted writing time for this book and Marist College for Carol's research course release. This project would not have been possible without these supports.

Lynnette would like to specifically thank Mathews and Tuntu Mazibuko for opening their home to me during the writing of this book. Tuntu, I thank you explicitly for your love, laughter, sisterhood, and all the joy you bring in my world. To the triplets, Naledi, Sechaba, and Maxwell, I thank you for all your bubbly energy and companionship as you sat next to me while writing this book. And to the pooch, Cookie, for all your overall "crazy" and belly rubs—you bring such laughter to the house.

I would also like to thank my crew: Emery Petchauer, Kira Baker-Doyle, Sonia Rosen, Decoteau Irby, and Laura Porterfield for your continual support, encouragement, and friendship. You have all strengthened and stretched me to be a better scholar, and I consider your friendship to be invaluable. I would also like to give big ups to Brenda Leake, Tabitha Dell'Angelo, Lauren Madden,

Eileen Heddy, and MinSoo Bossard-Kim. I could not ask for better colleagues in this world.

Lastly, I would like to thank my "kiddos" at New Hope Children's Home in Kenya. You all kept me grounded during the writing of this book. I am so blessed that I got to play a role in your lives, as you have all made a huge imprint on my life. And thank you to Robert Njoka Gachoki for your constant love, reassurance, and helping me to live my life outside the box. On the days I wanted to run from writing, you continued to push me to write just a little more, and I am grateful for that. I love you to the moon and back (#oldandtoothless). And most importantly, thank you to Carol Rinke for being an amazing work partner and friend. I have really cherished our research partnership that has lasted over thirteen years, and I look forward to many, many more years.

Carol would like to thank the many friends, colleagues, and former students from across the country who helped us to connect with these teacher leavers. We have mentioned throughout the book that one of the most challenging aspects of this study was simply identifying the teachers themselves. I reached out to colleagues and former students far and wide to help identify teachers who have left the classroom. Thank you for returning my call Andrew Arenge, Brian Baldwin, Paul Hutchison, Nancy Lee, Dan Levin, John McAdam, Joe Miller, and Jennie Pagano.

Thank you also to the Marist College Education Department for your collegiality and support through this process. In particular, I want to thank the members of the Research Collaboration Group who provided vital insights on earlier versions of this work: Jane Bean-Folkes, Nora Brakas, Wendy Gladstone-Brown, Jan Stivers, Zsuzsanna Szabo, Kathy Trela, and Katya Vigil. Thank you also to all the members of the Creating an Inclusive Community group—you can see our conversations echoed throughout this work.

Lynnette—thank you for your enthusiasm, your amazing networking skills, and for always thinking of the next step. My career would be so different if we had not met in San Francisco thirteen years ago. And finally, thank you to my family, Michael, Coby, and Noah Rinke, for your unwavering support and endless laughter.

Parts of the introduction and chapter 1 were originally published as "Insights from Teacher Leavers: Push and Pull in Career Development," by Carol R. Rinke and Lynnette Mawhinney, *Teaching Education* 28, no. 10 (March 2017): 1–17. https://www.tandfonline.com.

Most of chapter 7 has been published in "I Just Feel So Guilty: The Role of Emotions in Former Urban Teachers' Career Paths," by Lynnette Mawhinney and Carol R. Rinke, *Urban Education* 53, no. 9 (November 2017): 1079–1101, published by SAGE Publishing. All rights reserved.

References

Acheson, Kris, Justin Taylor, and Kera Luna. 2016. "The Burnout Spiral: The Emotion Labor of Five Rural U.S. Foreign Language Teachers. *Modern Language Journal* 100 (2): 522–537.

Allen, Ayana, Lakia M. Scott, and Chance W. Lewis. 2013. "Racial Microaggressions and African American and Hispanic Students in Urban Schools: A Call for Culturally Affirming Education." *Interdisciplinary Journal of Teaching and Learning* 3 (2): 117–129.

Allen, Quaylan. 2013. "'They Think Minority Means Lesser Than': Black Middle-Class Sons and Fathers Resisting Microaggressions in the School." *Urban Education* 48 (2): 171–197.

Amodio, David M., Patricia G. Devine, and Eddie Harmon-Jones. 2007. "A Dynamic Model of Guilt: Implications for Motivation and Self-Regulation in the Context of Prejudice." *Psychological Science* 18 (6): 524–530.

Andrews, Dorinda J. Carter. 2012. "Black Achievers' Experiences with Racial Spotlighting and Ignoring in a Predominantly White High School." *Teachers College Record* 114 (10): 1–46.

Atkinson, Robert. 1998. *The Life Story Interview.* Thousand Oaks, CA: Sage Publications.

Bacolod, Marigee P. 2007a. "Do Alternative Opportunities Matter? The Role of Female Labor Markets in the Decline of Teacher Quality." *Review of Economics and Statistics* 89(4): 737–751.

———. 2007b. "Who Teaches and Where They Choose to Teach: College Graduates of the 1990s." *Educational Evaluation and Policy Analysis* 29 (3): 155–168.

Barber, Michael, and Mona Mourshed. 2007. *How the World's Best-Performing School Systems Come Out on Top.* New York: McKinsey & Company.

Barnes, Gary, Edward Crowe, and Benjamin Schaefer. 2007. "The Cost of Teacher Turnover in Five School Districts: A Pilot Study." *National Commission on Teaching and America's Future.* https://nctaf.org/wp-content/uploads/2012/01/NCTAF-Cost-of-Teacher-Turnover-2007-full-report.pdf.

Barthelemy, Ramón S., Melinda McCormick, and Charles Henderson. 2016. "Gender Discrimination in Physics and Astronomy: Graduate Student Experiences of Sexism and Gender Microaggressions." *Physical Review Physics Education Research* 12 (2): 20119.

Bennett, Christine I., Lynn M. McWhorter, and John A. Kuykendall. 2006. "Will I Ever Teach? Latino and African American Students' Perspectives on PRAXIS I." *American Educational Research Journal* 43 (3): 531–575.

Berk, Ronald A. 2017. "Microaggressions Trilogy: Part 1. Why Do Microaggressions Matter?" *Journal of Faculty Development* 31 (1): 63–73.

Berlak, Ann, and Sekani Moyenda. 2001. *Taking It Personally: Racism in the Classroom from Kindergarten to College.* Philadelphia: Temple University Press.

Berry, Barnett, Diana Montgomery, and Jon Snyder. 2008. *Urban Teacher Residency Models and Institutes of Higher Education: Implications for Teacher Preparation.* National Council for Accreditation of Teacher Education and Center for Teaching Quality.

Biklen, Sari Knopp. 1995. *School Work: Gender and the Cultural Construction of Teaching.* New York: Teachers College Press.

Boggess, Laurence B. 2010. "Tailoring New Urban Teachers for Character and Activism." *American Educational Research Journal* 47 (1): 65–95.

Boysen, Guy A. 2012. "Teacher and Student Perceptions of Microaggressions in College Classrooms." *College Teaching* 60 (3): 122–129.

Brennan, Karen. 2006. "The Managed Teacher: Emotional Labour, Education, and Technology." *Educational Insights* 10 (2): 55–65.

Brunetti, Gerald J. 2006. "Resilience under Fire: Perspectives on the Work of Experienced, Inner City High School Teachers in the United States." *Teaching and Teacher Education* 22 (7): 812–825.

Bryan, Nathaniel, and Jamison K. Browder. 2013. "'Are You Sure You Know What You Are Doing?'—The Lived Experiences of an African American Male Kindergarten Teacher." *Interdisciplinary Journal of Teaching and Learning* 3 (3): 142–158.

Buchanan, J. D. 2009. "Where Are They Now? Ex-Teachers Tell Their Life-Work Stories." *Issues in Educational Research,* 19 (1): 13.

Buckley, Jack, Mark Schneider, and Yi Shang. 2005. "Fix It and They Might Stay: School Facility Quality and Teacher Retention in Washington, DC." *Teachers College Record* 107 (5): 1107–1123.

Budge, Claire, Jennifer Carryer, and Sue Wood. 2003. "Health Correlates of Autonomy, Control and Professional Relationships in the Nursing Work Environment." *Journal of Advanced Nursing* 42 (3): 260–268. doi: 10.1046/j.1365-2648.2003.02615.x.

Bulman, Robert. 2002. "Teachers in the 'Hood: Hollywood's Middle-Class Fantasy." *Urban Review* 34(3): 251–276.

Carroll, Thomas G. 2007. "Policy Brief: The High Cost of Teacher Turnover." *National Commission on Teaching and America's Future.* https://nctaf.org/wp-content/uploads/NCTAFCostofTeacherTurnoverpolicybrief.pdf.

Carroll, Thomas G., and Elizabeth Foster. 2010. "Who Will Teach? Experience Matters." *National Commission on Teaching and America's Future*: 510. https://nctaf.org/wp-content/uploads/2012/01/NCTAF-Who-Will-Teach-Experience-Matters-2010-Report.pdf.

Chambers, Crystal Renée. 2011/2012. "Candid Reflections on the Departure of Black Women Faculty from Academe in the United States." *Negro Educational Review* 62/63 (1–4): 233–260.

Clandinin, D. Jean, Julie Long, Lee Schaefer, C. Aiden Downey, Pam Steeves, Eliza Pinnegar, Sue McKenzie Robblee, and Sheri Wnuk. 2015. "Early Career Teacher Attrition: Intentions of Teachers Beginning." *Teaching Education* 26 (1): 1–16.

Clifford, Geraldine Jonçich. 1989. "Man/Woman/Teacher: Gender, Family, and Career in American Educational History." In *American Teachers: Histories of a Profession at*

Work, edited by Donald R. Warren, 293–343. New York: American Educational Research Association.

Council for the Accreditation of Educator Preparation. 2013. *2013 CAEP Standards.* Washington DC: Author.

Council for the Accreditation of Educator Preparation. 2015. *CAEP Evidence Guide.* Washington DC: Author.

Council on Social Work Education. 2015. *Educational Policy and Accreditation Standards* Alexandria, VA: Commission on Accreditation and Educational Policy.

Cuban, Larry. 1990. "Reforming Again, Again, and Again." *Educational Researcher* 19 (1): 3–13.

Çukur, Cem Safak. 2009. "The Development of the Teacher Emotional Labor Scale (TELS): Validity and Reliability." *Educational Sciences: Theory and Practice* 9 (2): 559–574.

Cushman, Penni. 2005. "Let's Hear It from the Males: Issues Facing Male Primary School Teachers." *Teaching and Teacher Education* 21 (3): 227–240.

Darling-Hammond, Linda. 2015. *The Flat World and Education: How America's Commitment to Equity Will Determine our Future.* New York: Teachers College Press.

Darling-Hammond, Linda, and Ann Lieberman. 2012. "Teacher Education around the World: What Can We Learn from International Practice?" In *Teacher Education around the World: Changing Policies and Practices*, edited by Linda Darling-Hammond and Ann Lieberman, 151–169. New York: Routledge.

Darling Hammond, Linda, and Richard Rothman. 2011. *Teacher and Leader Effectiveness in High-Performing Education Systems.* Washington, DC: Alliance for Excellent Education and Stanford, CA: Stanford Center for Opportunity Policy in Education.

Dávila, Brianne. 2015. "Critical Race Theory, Disability Microaggressions and Latina/o Student Experiences in Special Education." *Race, Ethnicity, and Education* 18 (4): 443–468.

Davis, Joan, and Sandra M. Wilson. 2000. "Principals' Efforts to Empower Teachers: Effects on Teacher Motivation and Job Satisfaction and Stress." *Clearing House* 73 (6): 349–353.

Day, Christopher. 2017. *Teachers' Worlds and Work: Understanding Complexity, Building Quality.* London: Routledge.

Day, Christopher, and Qing Gu. 2009. "Veteran Teachers: Commitment, Resilience and Quality Retention." *Teachers and Teaching: Theory and Practice* 15(4): 441–457.

———. 2010. *The New Lives of Teachers.* New York: Routledge.

———. 2013. *Resilient Teachers, Resilient Schools: Building and Sustaining Quality in Testing Times.* New York: Routledge.

Day, Christopher, Pam Sammons, and Gordon Stobart. 2007. *Teachers Matter: Connecting Lives, Work and Effectiveness.* Maidenhead: Open University Press.

DeAngelis, Karen J., and Jennifer B. Presley. 2011. "Toward a More Nuanced Understanding of New Teacher Attrition." *Education and Urban Society* 43 (5): 598–626.

DeCuir-Gunby, Jessica T., and Norris W. Gunby Jr. 2016. "Racial Microaggressions in the Workplace: A Critical Race Analysis of the Experiences of African American Educators." *Urban Education* 51 (4): 390–414.

Deffenbaugh, W. S. 1925. "Some Recent Movements in City School Systems." Washington, DC: Department of Interior, Bureau of Education.

Denzin, Norman K., and Yvonna S. Lincoln. 2001. "Paradigms and Perspectives in Contention." In *The SAGE Handbook of Qualitative Research*, edited by Norman K. Denzin and Yvonna S. Lincoln, 91–96. Thousand Oaks, CA: Sage Publishing.

Desimone, Laura, Andrew C. Porter, Michael S. Garet, Suk Yoon Kwang, and Beatrice F. Birman. 2002. "Effects of Professional Development on Teachers' Instruction: Results from a Three-Year Longitudinal Study." *Educational Evaluation and Policy Analysis* 24 (2): 81–112.

Dinham, Steve, and Catherine Scott. 1998. "A Three Domain Model of Teacher and School Executive Career Satisfaction." *Journal of Educational Administration* 36 (4): 362–378.

———. 2000. "Moving into the Third, Outer Domain of Teacher Satisfaction" *Journal of Educational Administration* 38 (4): 379–396.

Donaldson, Morgaen L. 2005. "Building a Better Career Ladder: A New Spin on Old Reforms May Help Keep Today's Teachers in the Classroom." In *Recruiting, Retaining, and Supporting Highly Qualified Teachers*, edited by Caroline Chauncey, 77–87. Cambridge, MA: Harvard Educational Press.

Donaldson, Morgaen L., and Susan Moore Johnson. 2010. "The Price of Misassignment: The Role of Teaching Assignments in Teach for America Teachers' Exit from Low-Income Schools and the Teaching Profession." *Educational Evaluation and Policy Analysis* 32 (2): 299–323.

Donaldson, Morgaen L., Susan Moore Johnson, Cheryl L. Kirkpatrick, William H. Marinell, Jennifer L. Steele, and Stacy Agee Szczesiul. 2008. "Angling for Access, Bartering for Change: How Second-Stage Teachers Experience Differentiated Roles in Schools." *Teachers College Record* 110 (5): 1088–1114.

Downing, Dick, Ruth Watson, Fiona Johnson, Pippa Lord, Megan Jones, and Mary Ashworth. 2004. "Sabbaticals for Teachers: An Evaluation of a Scheme Offering Sabbaticals for Experienced Teachers Working in Challenging Schools." *London, DfES RR547*.

Drudy, S., Martin, M., Woods, M., and O'Flynn, J. 2005. *Men and the Classroom: Gender Imbalances in Teaching*. New York: Routledge.

Dworkin, Anthony Gary. 1980. "The Changing Demography of Public School Teachers: Some Implications for Faculty Turnover in Urban Areas." *Sociology of Education*: 65–73.

Dwyer, Peter, and Johanna Wyn. 2007. *Youth, Education and Risk: Facing the Future*. New York: Routledge.

Ehrich, Lisa C., Brian Hansford, and Lee Tennent. 2004. "Formal Mentoring Programs in Education and Other Professions: A Review of the Literature." *Educational Administration Quarterly* 40 (4): 518–540. doi:10.1177/0013161X04267118.

Endo, R. 2015. "How Asian American Female Teachers Experience Racial Microaggressions from Pre-service Preparation to Their Professional Careers." *Urban Review* 47 (4): 601–625.

Families and Work Institute. 2007. "Generations and Gender in the Workplace." New York: Author.

Farkas, Steve, Jean Johnson, and Ann Duffett. 2003. *Stand by Me: What Teachers Really Think about Unions, Merit Pay, and Other Professional Matters*. New York: Public Agenda.

Farouk, Shaalan. 2012. "What Can the Self-Conscious Emotion of Guilt Tell Us about Primary School Teachers' Moral Purpose and the Relationships They Have with Their Pupils?" *Teachers and Teaching* 18 (4): 491–507.

Feiman-Nemser, Sharon. 2001. "From Preparation to Practice: Designing a Continuum to Strengthen and Sustain Teaching." *Teachers College Record* 103 (6): 1013–1055.

Firestone, William. 2014. "Teacher Evaluation Policy and Conflicting Theories of Motivation." *Educational Researcher* 43 (2): 100–107.

Fisher, Edith M. 2008. "USA Stratified Monopoly: A Simulation Game about Social Class Stratification." *Teaching Sociology* 36 (3): 272–282.

Flores, Maria Assunção, and Christopher Day. 2006. "Contexts Which Shape and Reshape New Teachers' Identities: A Multi-Perspective Study." *Teaching and Teacher Education* 22 (2): 219–232.

Follins, Lourdes D., Lisa K. Paler, and José E. Nanin. 2015. "Creating and Implementing a Faculty Interest Group for Historically Underrepresented Faculty." *Community College Journal of Research and Practice* 39 (9): 839–851.

Fowler, William J. Jr., and Kavita Mittapalli. 2006. "Where Do Public School Teachers Go When They Leave Teaching?" *ERS Spectrum* 24 (4): 4–12.

Francis, Dennis A, and Finn Reygan. 2016. "'Let's See If It Won't Go Away by Itself': LGBT Microaggressions among Teachers in South Africa." *Education as Change* 20 (3): 180–201.

Freedman, Sarah Warshauer, and Deborah Appleman. 2008. "'What Else Would I Be Doing?': Teacher Identity and Teacher Retention in Urban Schools." *Teacher Education Quarterly* 35 (3): 109–126.

Galletta, Maura, Igor Portoghese, and Adalgisa Battistelli. 2011. "Intrinsic Motivation, Job Autonomy and Turnover Intention in the Italian Healthcare: The Mediating Role of Affective Commitment." *Journal of Management Research* 3 (2): 1.

Garcia, Cynthia Martinez, John R. Slate, and Carmen Tejeda Delgado. 2009. "Salary and Ranking and Teacher Turnover: A Statewide Study." *International Journal of Education Policy and Leadership* 4 (7): 1–8.

Goings, Ramon B., and Margarita Bianco. 2016. "It's Hard to Be Who You Don't See: An Exploration of Black Male High School Students' Perspectives on Becoming Teachers." *Urban Review* 48 (4): 628–646.

Goldring, Rebecca, Soheyla Taie, and Minsun Riddles. 2014. "Teacher Attrition and Mobility: Results from the 2012–13 Teacher Follow-Up Survey. First look. NCES 2014-077." *National Center for Education Statistics.*

Goldstein, Dana. 2014. *The Teacher Wars: A History of America's Most Embattled Profession*. New York: Anchor.

Goodson, Ivor F., and Patricia J. Sikes. 2001. *Life History Research in Educational Settings: Learning from Lives*. Buckingham: Open University Press.

Gray, Lucinda, and Soheyla Taie. 2015. "Public School Teacher Attrition and Mobility in the First Five Years: Results from the First through Fifth Waves of the 2007–08 Beginning Teacher Longitudinal Study. First look. NCES 2015-337." *National Center for Education Statistics.*

Grissmer, David W., Ann Flanagan, Jennifer H. Kawata, Stephanie Williamson, and Tom LaTourrette. 2000. *Improving Student Achievement: What State NAEP Test Scores Tell Us*. Rand Corporation.

Grossman, Pamela. 2005. "Research on Pedagogical Approaches in Teacher Education." In *Studying Teacher Education*, edited by Marilyn Cochran-Smith and Kenneth Zeichner, 425–476. Mahwah, NJ: Lawrence Erlbaum.

Hancock, Carl B. 2016. "Is the Grass Greener? Current and Former Music Teachers' Perceptions a Year After Moving to a Different School or Leaving the Classroom." *Journal of Research in Music Education* 63 (4): 421–438.

Hancock, Carl B., and Lisa Scherff. 2010. "Who Will Stay and Who Will Leave? Predicting Secondary English Teacher Attrition Risk." *Journal of Teacher Education* 61 (4): 328–338.

Hanushek, Eric A. 2007. "The Single Salary Schedule and Other Issues of Teacher Pay." *Peabody Journal of Education* 82 (4): 574–586.

Hargreaves, Andy. 1994. *Changing Teachers, Changing Times: Teachers' Work and Culture in the Postmodern Age*. New York: Teachers College Press.

———. 1998. "The Emotional Practice of Teaching." *Teaching and Teacher Education* 14 (8): 835–854.

Hargreaves, Andy, and Michael Fullan. 2012. *Professional Capital: Transforming Teaching in Every School*. New York: Teachers College Press.

Hargreaves, Linda. 2009. "The Status and Prestige of Teachers and Teaching." In *International Handbook of Research on Teachers and Teaching* edited by L. J. Saha and A. G. Dworkin, 217–229. New York: Springer.

Harland, John, and Kay Kinder. 1997. "Teachers' Continuing Professional Development: Framing a Model of Outcomes." *British Journal of In-Service Education* 23 (1): 71–84.

Helms, Jenifer V. 1998. "Science—and Me: Subject Matter and Identity in Secondary School Science Teachers." *Journal of Research in Science Teaching* 35 (7): 811–834.

Hemms, Kerry, and Graham White. 2017. *Teacher's Field Guide: 7 Truths about Teaching to Help You Start off Strong, Avoid Burnout, and Stay in Love with Teaching*. New York: Morgan James Publishing.

Henfield, Malik S. 2011. "Black Male Adolescents Navigating Microaggressions in a Traditionally White Middle School: A Qualitative Study." *Journal of Multicultural Counseling and Development* 39 (3): 141.

Henry, Gary T., Kevin C. Bastian, and C. Kevin Fortner. 2011. "Stayers and Leavers: Early-Career Teacher Effectiveness and Attrition." *Educational Researcher* 40 (6): 271–280.

Henry, Gary T., C. Kevin Fortner, and Kevin C. Bastian. 2012. "The Effects of Experience and Attrition for Novice High-School Science and Mathematics Teachers." *Science* 335(6072): 1118–1121.

Herman, Keith C., and Wendy M. Reinke. 2014. *Stress Management for Teachers: A Proactive Guide*. New York: Guilford Publications.

Hochschild, Arlie Russell. 2012. *The Managed Heart: Commercialization of Human Feeling*. Berkeley: University of California Press.

Hope, Elan C., Micere Keels, and Myles I. Durkee. 2016. "Participation in Black Lives Matter and Deferred Action for Childhood Arrivals: Modern Activism among Black and Latino College Students." *Journal of Diversity in Higher Education* 9 (3): 203.

Hotchkins, B. 2016. "African American Males Navigate Racial Microaggression." *Teachers College Record* 118: 1–36.

Hoyle, Eric. 2001. "Teaching Prestige, Status and Esteem." *Educational Management & Administration* 29 (2): 139–152.

HSBC. 2016. "Expat Explorer: Achieving Ambitions Abroad Global Report."

Hu, Winnie. 2010. "Teachers Facing Weakest Market in Years." *New York Times*, May 19.

Huber, Lindsay Pérez. 2011. "Discourses of Racist Nativism in California Public Education: English Dominance as Racist Nativist Microaggressions." *Educational Studies* 47 (4): 379–401.

Huberman, Michael. 1989. "The Professional Life Cycle of Teachers." *Teachers College Record*: 31–57.

———. 1993. *The Lives of Teachers*. London: Cassell.

Huntspon, Allen, and George Howell. 2012. "Black Male Teachers Becoming Extinct." *Cable News Network*. Retrieved from http://inamerica.blogs.cnn.com/2012/02/23/black-male-teachers-becoming-extinct/.

Imazeki, Jennifer. 2002. "Teacher Attrition and Mobility in Urban Districts: Evidence from Wisconsin." In *Fiscal Policy in Urban Education*, edited by Christopher Roellke and Jennifer King Rice, 119–136. Greenwich, CT: Information Age Publishers.

Ingersoll, Richard M. 1999. "The Problem of Underqualified Teachers in American Secondary Schools." *Educational Researcher* 28 (2): 26–37.

———. 2003. "Is There Really a Teacher Shortage?" University of Washington: Center for the Study of Teaching and Policy.

Ingersoll, Richard M., and Lisa Merrill. 2012. "Seven Trends: The Transformation of the Teaching Force." University of Pennsylvania Graduate School of Education Publications. http://repository.upenn.edu/cgi/viewcontent.cgi?article=1261&context=gse_pubs.

Ingersoll, Richard M., and David Perda. 2010. "Is the Supply of Mathematics and Science Teachers Sufficient." *American Educational Research Journal* 47 (3): 563–594.

Institute of Healthcare Improvement. 2017. *Plan-Do-Study-Act (PDSA) Worksheet*. http://www.ihi.org/resources/Pages/Tools/PlanDoStudyActWorksheet.aspx.

Irby, Decoteau J. 2015. "Urban Is Floating Face Down in the Mainstream: Using Hip-Hop-Based Education Research to Resurrect 'the Urban' in Urban Education." *Urban Education* 50 (1): 7–30.

Irving, Debby 2014. *Waking Up White: And Finding Myself in the Story of Race*. Chicago: Elephant Room Press.

Jo, Seog Hun. 2014. "Teacher Commitment: Exploring Associations with Relationships and Emotions." *Teaching and Teacher Education* 43: 120–130.

Johnson, Jean, and Ann Duffett. 2003. *An Assessment of Survey Data on Attitudes about Teaching Including the Views of Parents, Administrators, Teachers and the General Public*. New York: Public Agenda.

Johnson, Susan Moore. 2007. *Finders and Keepers: Helping New Teachers Survive and Thrive in Our Schools*. San Francisco: Jossey-Bass.

Johnson, Susan Moore, Matthew A. Kraft, and John P. Papay. 2012. "How Context Matters in High-Need Schools: The Effects of Teachers' Working Conditions on Their Professional Satisfaction and Their Students' Achievement." *Teachers College Record* 114 (10): 1–39.

Kaiser, Ashley. 2011. *Beginning Teacher Attrition and Mobility: Results from the First through Third Waves of the 2007–2008 Beginning Teacher Longitudinal Study. First Look. NCES 2011–318*. Washington DC: National Center for Educational Statistics.

Keller, Bess. 2007. "Oft-Cited Statistic Likely Inaccurate." *Education Week* 26 (41): 30.

Kelley, Todd R. 2016. "Postcards from a Road Trip to Innovation: One Professor's Sabbatical." *Technology and Engineering Teacher* 76 (3): 26–30.

Keogh, Jayne, Susie Garvis, and Donna Lee Pendergast. 2010. "Plugging the Leaky Bucket: The Need to Develop Resilience in Novice Middle Years Teachers." *Middle Years Educator* 8 (2): 17–26.

Kohli, Rita, and Daniel G Solórzano. 2012. "Teachers, Please Learn Our Names! Racial Microaggressions and the K–12 Classroom." *Race, Ethnicity, and Education* 15 (4): 441–462.

Kraehe, Amelia M. 2015. "Sounds of Silence: Race and Emergent Counter-narratives of Art Teacher Identity." *Studies in Art Education* 56 (3): 199–213.

Ladd, Helen F. 2011. "Teachers' Perceptions of Their Working Conditions: How Predictive of Planned and Actual Teacher Movement?" *Educational Evaluation and Policy Analysis* 33 (2): 235–261.

Ladson-Billings, Gloria. 2001. *Crossing over to Canaan: The Journey of New Teachers in Diverse Classrooms*. San Francisco: Jossey-Bass.

Lamb, R. E. 1983. "Guilt, Shame, and Morality." *Philosophy and Phenomenological Research* 4 3(3): 329–346.

Leithwood, Kenneth A. 1990. "The Principal's Role in Teacher Development." In *Changing School Culture through Staff Development*, edited by Bruce Joyce, 71–90. Alexandria, VA: Association for Supervision and Curriculum.

Lent, Robert W., Steven D. Brown, and Gail Hackett. 1994. "Toward a Unifying Social Cognitive Theory of Career and Academic Interest, Choice, and Performance." *Journal of Vocational Behavior* 45: 79–122.

Lester, Jaime, Aoi Yamanaka, and Brice Struthers. 2016. "Gender Microaggressions and Learning Environments: The Role of Physical Space in Teaching Pedagogy and Communication." *Community College Journal of Research and Practice* 40 (11): 909–926.

Lewis, Chance W., and Ivory A. Toldson, eds. 2013. *Black Male Teachers*. Bingley, UK: Emerald Group Publishing Limited.

Liang, Xiaoyan. 2000. *Teacher Pay in 12 Latin American Countries: How Does Teacher Pay Compare to Other Professions? What Determines Teacher Pay? Who Are the Teachers?* World Bank, Latin America and the Caribbean Regional Office.

Littrell, Peggy C., Bonnie S. Billingsley, and Lawrence H. Cross. 1994. "The Effects of Principal Support on Special and General Educators' Stress, Job Satisfaction, School Commitment, Health, and Intent to Stay in Teaching." *Journal for Special Educators* 15 (5): 297–310.

Lortie, Dan C. 1975. *Schoolteacher: A Sociological Study*. Chicago: University of Chicago Press.

Lynn, Marvin. 2002. "Critical Race Theory and the Perspectives of Black Men Teachers in the Los Angeles Public Schools." *Equity & Excellence in Education* 35 (2): 119–130.

———. 2006. "Dancing between Two Worlds: A Portrait of the Life of a Black Male Teacher in South Central LA." *International Journal of Qualitative Studies in Education* 19 (2): 221–242.

Macdonald, Doune. 1999. "Teacher Attrition: A Review of Literature." *Teaching and Teacher Education* 15 (8): 835–848.

MacMillan, Robert, and Matthew J. Meyer. 2006. "Inclusion and Guilt: The Emotional Fallout for Teachers." *Exceptionality Education Canada* 16 (1): 25–43.

Maher, Frances A., and Janie Victoria Ward. 2002. *Gender and Teaching*. Mahwah, NJ: Lawrence Erlbaum Associates.

Malloy, Courtney L., and Priscilla Wohlstetter. 2003. "Working Conditions in Charter Schools: What's the Appeal for Teachers?" *Education and Urban Society* 35 (2): 219–241.

Margolis, Jason. 2008. "What Will Keep Today's Teachers Teaching? Looking for a Hook as a New Career Cycle Emerges." *Teachers College Record* 110 (1): 160–194.

Markow, Dana, Lara Macia, and Helen Lee. 2013. *The MetLife Survey of the American Teacher: Challenges for School Leadership*. New York: Metropolitan Life Insurance Company.

Maslach, Christina, Wilmar B. Schaufeli, and Michael P. Leiter. 2001. "Job Burnout." *Annual Review of Psychology* 52 (1): 397–422.

Mawhinney, Lynnette. 2008a. "Coping with Stress through Validation: A Tool of the Teaching Trade." *Journal of Ethnographic & Qualitative Research* 2 (4): 246–254.

———. 2008b. "Laugh So You Don't Cry: Teachers Combating Isolation in Schools through Humour and Social Support." *Ethnography and Education* 3 (2): 195–209.

———. 2014. *We Got Next: Urban Education and the Next Generation of Black Teachers*. New York: Peter Lang.

Mawhinney, Lynnette, Carol R. Rinke, and Gloria Park. 2012. "Being and Becoming a Teacher: How African American and White Preservice Teachers Envision their Future Roles as Teacher Advocates." *New Educator* 8 (4): 321–344.

McCarthy, Christopher J., Richard G. Lambert, Megan O'Donnell, and Lauren T. Melendres. 2009. "The Relation of Elementary Teachers' Experience, Stress, and Coping Resources to Burnout Symptoms." *Elementary School Journal* 109 (3): 282–300.

McIntyre, Joanna. 2010. "Why They Sat Still: The Ideas and Values of Long-Serving Teachers in Challenging Inner-City Schools in England." *Teachers and Teaching: Theory and Practice* 16 (5): 595–614.

Mellor, David. 2004. "Responses to Racism: A Taxonomy of Coping Styles Used by Aboriginal Australians." *American Journal of Orthopsychiatry* 74 (1): 56–71.

Michael, Ali. 2015. *Raising Race Questions: Whiteness & Inquiry in Education.* New York: Teachers College Press.

Miller, Michael T, Kang Bai, and Richard E Newman. 2012. "A Critical Examination of Sabbatical Application Policies: Implications for Academic Leaders." *College Quarterly* 15 (2): n2.

Milner, Richard H. 2012. "But What Is Urban Education?" *Urban Education* 47 (3): 556–561.

Moore, Donald R., and Arthur A. Hyde. 1980. "An Analysis of Staff Development Programs and Their Costs in Three Urban School Districts." *National Institution of Education.*

Mulholland, Rosie, Andy McKinlay, and John Sproule. 2017. "Teachers in Need of Space: The Content and Changing Context of Work." *Educational Review* 69 (2): 181–200.

Murnane, Richard J., and Randall J. Olsen. 1990. "The Effects of Salaries and Opportunity Costs on Length of Stay in Teaching: Evidence from North Carolina." *Journal of Human Resources*: 106–124.

National Association of Social Workers. 1996. *Code of Ethics.* Washington DC: Author.

National Center for Educational Statistics. 2008. *Public School Teacher, BIE School Teacher, and Private School Teacher Data Files.* Washington DC: U.S. Department of Education, National Center for Educational Statistics, Schools and Staffing Survey (SASS).

National Center for Educational Statistics. 2016. "Number and Percentage Distribution of Teachers in Public and Private Elementary and Secondary Schools, by Selecting Teacher Characteristics: Selected Years, 1987–88 through 2011–12." https://nces.ed.gov/programs/digest/d13/tables/dt13_209.10.asp.

National Conference of State Legislatures. 2016. "No Time to Lose: How to Build a World-Class Education System State by State." http://www.ncsl.org/documents/educ/Edu_International_Final_V2.pdf.

National Council on Teaching and America's Future. 2007. "Policy Brief: The High Cost of Teacher Turnover." Washington DC: Author.

Nettles, Michael T., Linda H. Scatton, Jonathan H. Steinberg, and Linda L. Tyler. 2011. "Performance and Passing Rate Differences of African American and White Prospective Teachers on Praxis™ Examinations: A Joint Project of the National Education Association (NEA) and Educational Testing Service (ETS)." *ETS Research Report Series* 2011 (1).

Nias, Jennifer. 1996. "Thinking about Feeling: The Emotions in Teaching." *Cambridge Journal of Education* 26 (3): 293–306.

Nieto, Sonia. 2001. "What Keeps Teachers Going? And Other Thoughts on the Future of Public Education." *Equity and Excellence in Education* 34 (1): 6–15.

———. 2003. *What Keeps Teachers Going?* New York: Teachers College Press.

———. 2005. *Why We Teach.* New York: Teachers College Press.

Oakes, Jeannie, Rebecca Joseph, and Kate Muir. 2004. "Access and Achievement in Mathematics and Science: Inequalities that Endure and Change." In *Handbook of Research on Multicultural Education*, edited by James A. Banks and Cherry A. McGee Banks, 69–90. San Francisco: Jossey-Bass.

O'Brien, Leigh M., and Martha Schillaci. 2002. "Why Do I Want to Teach, Anyway? Utilizing Autobiography in Teacher Education." *Teaching Education* 13 (1): 25–40.

OECD. 2009. *Creating Effective Teaching and Learning Environments: First Results from TALIS.* Paris: OECD Publishing.

OECD. 2005. *Teachers Matter: Attracting, Developing, and Retaining Effective Teachers.* Paris: OECD Publishing.

Olsen, Brad. 2008. "How Reasons for Entry into the Profession Illuminate Teacher Identity Development." *Teacher Education Quarterly* 35 (3): 23–40.

Olsen, Brad, and Lauren Anderson. 2007. "Courses of Action: A Qualitative Investigation into Urban Teacher Retention and Career Development." *Urban Education* 42 (1): 5–29.

Otto, Linda R, and Michael Kroth. 2011. "An Examination of the Benefits and Costs of Sabbatical Leave for General Higher Education, Industry, and Professional-Technical/Community College Environments." *Journal of STEM Teacher Education* 48 (3): 21–43.

Owens, John. 2013. *Confessions of a Bad Teacher: The Shocking Truth from the Front Lines of American Public Education.* Sourcebooks, Inc.

Papay, John P. 2007. *The Teaching Workforce.* Washington DC: The Aspen Institute.

Park, Gloria. 2009. "I Listened to Korean Society. I Always Heard that Women Should Be This Way . . .": The Negotiation and Construction of Gendered Identities in Claiming a Dominant Language and Race in the United States." *Journal of Language, Identity, and Education* 8 (2–3): 174–190.

———. 2015. "Situating the Discourses of Privilege and Marginalization in the Lives of Two East Asian Women Teachers of English." *Race, Ethnicity, and Education* 18 (1): 108–133.

Patterson, Nancy C., Gillian H. Roehrig, and Julie A. Luft. 2003. "Running the Treadmill: Explorations of Beginning High School Science Teacher Turnover in Arizona." *High School Journal* 86 (4): 14–22.

Patton, Michael Quinn. 1990. *Qualitative Evaluation and Research Methods.* Newbury Park, CA: Sage Publications.

Peske, Heather G., Edward Liu, Susan Moore Johnson, David Kauffman, and Susan M. Kardos. 2001. "The Next Generation of Teachers: Changing Conceptions of a Career in Teaching." *Phi Delta Kappan* 83 (4): 304–311.

Petchauer, Emery. 2012. "Teacher Licensure Exams and Black Teacher Candidates: Toward New Theory and Promising Practice." *Journal of Negro Education* 81 (3): 252–267.

Pierce, Chester M., Jean V. Carew, Diane Pierce-Gonzalez, and Deborah Wills. 1978. "An Experiment in Racism: TV Commercials." In *Television and Education*, edited by Chester Pierce, 62–68. Beverly Hills, CA: Sage Publications.

Pierce, Stephanie. 2014. "Examining the Relationship between Collective Teacher Efficacy and the Emotional Intelligence of Elementary School Principals." *Journal of School Leadership* 24 (2): 311–335.

Plaisier, Inger, Jeanne G. M. de Bruijn, Ron de Graaf, Margreet ten Have, Aartjan T. F. Beekman, and Brenda W. J. H. Penninx. 2007. "The Contribution of Working Conditions and Social Support to the Onset of Depressive and Anxiety Disorders among Male and Female Employees." *Social Science & Medicine* 64 (2): 401–410. doi: http://dx.doi.org/10.1016/j.socscimed.2006.09.008.

Posse Foundation, The. "About Posse." 2014. https://www.possefoundation.org/about -posse.

Qazilbash, Emily Kalejs. 2007. "All for One, One for All? Early Career Teachers' Experiences with their Teachers' Unions in an Urban District." Annual Meeting of the American Educational Research Association, Chicago, IL.

Quartz, Karen Hunter, Andrew Thomas, Lauren Anderson, Katherine Masyn, Barraza Lyons, and Brad Olsen. 2008. "Careers in Motion: A Longitudinal Retention Study of Role Changing among Early-Career Urban Educators." *Teachers College Record* 110 (1): 218–250.

Quartz, Karen Hunter, Brad Olsen, Lauren Anderson, and Kimberly Barraza Lyons. 2010. *Making a Difference: Developing Meaningful Careers in Education.* Boulder, CO: Paradigm Publishers.

Rankin, Jenny Grant. 2016. *First Aid for Teacher Burnout: How You Can Find Peace and Success.* New York: Taylor & Francis.

Rinke, Carol R. 2008. "Understanding Teachers' Careers: Linking Professional Life to Professional Path." *Educational Research Review* 3 (1): 1–13.

———. 2009. "Finding Their Way On: Career Decision-Making Processes of Urban Science Teachers." *Science Education* 93 (6): 1096–1121.

———. 2013. "Teaching as Exploration? The Difficult Road Out of the Classroom." *Teaching and Teacher Education* 34: 98–106.

———. 2014. *Why Half of Teachers Leave the Classroom: Understanding Recruitment and Retention in Today's Schools.* Lanham, MD: Rowman & Littlefield Education.

Rinke, Carol R., and Lynnette Mawhinney. 2014. "Reconsidering Rapport with Urban Teachers: Negotiating Shifting Boundaries and Legitimizing Support." *International Journal of Research & Method in Education* 37 (1): 3–16.

Ripley, Amanda. 2016. "What America Can Learn about Smart Schools in Other Countries." *New York Times*, December 6.

Roberts, Ken, Stan C. Clark, and Claire Wallace. 1994. "Flexibility and Individualisation: A Comparison of Transitions into Employment in England and Germany." *Sociology* 28 (1): 31–54.

Ronfeldt, Matthew, Susanna Loeb, and James Wyckoff. 2013. "How Teacher Turnover Harms Student Achievement." *American Educational Research Journal* 50 (1): 4–36.

Rossi, Armando S. 1973. "Should It Be Compulsory? Sabbatical Leave for Teachers." *Massachusetts Teacher*: 10–11.

Rury, John L. 1989. "Who Became Teachers? The Social Characteristics of Teachers in American History." In *American Teachers: Histories of a Profession at Work*, edited by Donald Warren, 9–48, New York: Macmillan.

Sahlberg, P. 2010. *Finnish Lessons: What Can the World Learn from Educational Change in Finland?* New York: Teachers College Press.

Santoro, Doris A. 2011. "Teaching's Conscientious Objectors: Principled Leavers of High-Poverty Schools." *Teachers College Record* 113 (12): 2670–2704.

Santoro, Doris A., and Lisa Morehouse. 2011. "Teaching's Conscientious Objectors: Principled Leavers of High-Poverty Schools." *Teachers College Record* 113 (12): 2670–2704.

Savickas, Mark L. 2012. "Career Construction Theory and Practice." In *Career Development and Counseling: Putting Theory and Research to Work*, edited by Steven D. Brown and Robert W. Lent, 147–186. New York: Wiley.

Savickas, Mark L., Laura Nota, Jerome Rossier, Jean-Pierre Dauwalder, Maria Eduarda Duarte, Jean Guichard, Salvatore Soresi, Raoul Van Esbroeck, and Annelies EM Van Vianen. 2009. "Life Designing: A Paradigm for Career Construction in the 21st Century." *Journal of Vocational Behavior* 75 (3): 239–250.

Schaefer, Lee, C. Aiden Downey, and D. Jean Clandinin. 2014. "Shifting from Stories to Live by to Stories to Leave by: Early Career Teacher Attrition." *Teacher Education Quarterly* 41 (1): 9–27.

Schutz, Paul A., Kirsten C. Crowder, and Victoria E. White. 2001. "The Development of a Goal to Become a Teacher." *Journal of Educational Psychology* 93 (2): 299.

Schutz, Paul A., and Michalinos Zembylas, eds. 2009. *Advances in Teacher Emotion Research: The Impact on Teachers' Lives*. New York: Springer.

Schutz, Paul A., and Mikyoung Lee. 2014. "Teacher Emotion, Emotional Labor and Teacher Identity." *Utrecht Studies in Language and Communication* 27 (1): 169–186.

Scott, Catherine, Barbara Stone, and Steve Dinham. 2001. "I Love Teaching but . . . . International Patterns of Teacher Discontent." *Education Policy Analysis Archives*.

Sikes, Patricia J., Lynda Measor, and Peter Woods. 1985. *Teacher Careers: Crises and Continuities*. Lewes, UK: Falmer.

Singleton, Glenn E. 2014. *Courageous Conversations about Race: A Field Guide for Achieving Equity in Schools*. Thousand Oaks, CA: Corwin Press.

Sklarz, David P. 1991. "Keep Teachers on Their Toes with These 10 Retraining Tips." *Executive Educator* 13 (5): 26–29.

Smethem, Lindsey. 2007. "Retention and Intention in Teaching Careers: Will the New Generation Stay?" *Teachers and Teaching: Theory and Practice* 13 (5): 465–480.

Smith, William A., Jalil Bishop Mustaffa, Chantal M. Jones, Tommy J. Curry, and Walter R. Allen. 2016. "'You Make Me Wanna Holler and Throw Up Both My Hands!': Campus Culture, Black Misandric Microaggressions, and Racial Battle Fatigue." *International Journal of Qualitative Studies in Education* 29 (9): 1189–1209.

Smulyan, Lisa. 2004. "Choosing to Teach: Reflections on Gender and Social Change." *Teachers College Record* 106 (3): 513–543.

Snodgrass, Helen. 2010. "Perspectives of High-Achieving Women on Teaching." *New Educator* 6 (2): 135–152.

Solórzano, Daniel G., and Tara J. Yosso. 2002. "Critical Race Methodology: Counter-Storytelling as an Analytical Framework for Education Research." *Qualitative Inquiry* 8 (1): 23–44.

Song, Zhongying. 2008. "Current Situation of Job Burnout of Junior High School Teachers in Shangqiu Urban Areas and Its Relationship with Social Support." *Frontiers of Education in China* 3 (2): 295–309.

Stapleton, Lissa, and Natasha Croom. 2017. "Narratives of Black D/Deaf College Alum: Reflecting on Intersecting Microaggressions in College." *Journal of Student Affairs Research and Practice* 54 (1): 15–27.

Stern, Mark, and Amy Brown. 2016. "'It's 5:30. I'm Exhausted. And I Have to Go All the Way to F*%# ing Fishtown': Educator Depression, Activism, and Finding (Armed) Love in a Hopeless (Neoliberal) Place." *Urban Review* 48 (2): 333–354.

Suárez-Orozco, Carola, Saskias Casanova, Margary Martin, Dalal Katsiaficas, Veronica Cuellar, Naila Antonia Smith, and Sandra Isabel Dias. 2015. "Toxic Rain in Class

Classroom Interpersonal Microaggressions." *Educational Researcher* 44 (30): 151–160.

Sue, Derald Wing. 2010. *Microaggressions in Everyday Life: Race, Gender, and Sexual Orientation.* Hoboken, NJ: John Wiley & Sons, Inc.

———. 2016. *Race Talk and the Conspiracy of Silence: Understanding and Facilitating Difficult Dialogues on Race.* Hoboken: John Wiley & Sons.

Sue, Derald Wing, Christina M. Capodilupo, Gina C. Torino, Jennifer M. Bucceri, Aisha Holder, Kevin L. Nadal, and Marta Esquilin. 2007. "Racial Microaggressions in Everyday Life: Implications for Clinical Practice" *American Psychologist* 62 (4): 271.

Swanson, Jane L., and Paul A. Gore. 2000. "Advances in Vocational Psychology Theory and Research." In *Handbook of Counseling Psychology*, edited by Steven D. Brown and Robert W. Lent, 233–269. New York: John Wiley & Sons.

Tate, William F. 1997. "Critical Race Theory and Education: History, Theory, and Implications." *Review of Research in Education* 22 (1): 195–247.

Tatum, Beverly Daniel. 2017. *Why Are All the Black Kids Sitting Together in the Cafeteria? And Other Conversations about Race.* 5th ed. New York: Basic Books.

TeachNZ. 2017. "2018 Study Awards, Study Support Grants, and Sabbaticals." https://www.teachnz.govt.nz/teacher-awards/directory/primary-teachers-sabbatical/.

Tham, Pia, and Gabrielle Meagher. 2009. "Working in Human Services: How Do Experiences and Working Conditions in Child Welfare Social Work Compare?" *British Journal of Social Work* 39 (5): 807–827.

Tiedeman, David V., and Anna Miller-Tiedeman. 1985. "The Trend of Life in the Human Career." *Journal of Career Development* 11 (3): 221–250.

Tolbert, Sara, and Serina Eichelberger. 2016. "Surviving Teacher Education: A Community Cultural Capital Framework of Persistence." *Race, Ethnicity, and Education* 19 (5): 1025–1042.

Trigwell, Keith. 2012. "Relations between Teachers' Emotions in Teaching and Their Approaches to Teaching in Higher Education." *Instructional Science* 40 (3): 607–621.

Tyack, David B. 1974. *The One Best System: A History of American Urban Education.* Cambridge, MA: Harvard University Press.

U.S. Department of Education. 2016. *The State of Racial Diversity in the Educator Workforce*: 35. https://www2.ed.gov/rschstat/eval/highered/racial-diversity/state-racial-diversity-workforce.pdf, 2016.

van Veen, Klaas, Peter Sleegers, and Piet-Hein Van de Ven. 2005. "One Teacher's Identity, Emotions, and Commitment to Change: A Case Study into the Cognitive–Affective Processes of a Secondary School Teacher in the Context of Reforms. *Teaching and Teacher Education* 21 (8): 917–934.

Watt, Helen M. G., and Paul W. Richardson. 2008. "Motivations, Perceptions, and Aspirations concerning Teaching as a Career for Different Types of Beginning Teachers." *Learning and Instruction* 18 (5): 408–428.

Watt, Helen M. G., Paul W. Richardson, Uta Klusmann, Mareike Kunter, Beate Beyer, Ulrich Trautwein, and Jürgen Baumert. 2012. "Motivations for Choosing Teaching as a Career: An International Comparison Using the FIT-Choice Scale." *Teaching and Teacher Education* 28 (6): 791–805.

Weiner, Lois. 1990. "Preparing the Brightest for Urban Schools." *Urban Education* 25 (3): 258–273.

Whitman, David. 2008. "Sweating the Small Stuff: Inner-City Schools and the New Paternalism." Washington DC: Thomas B. Fordham Institute.

Wolfe, Paula. 2011. "Beyond the Literal: Microtransformations in a Secondary ESL Classroom." *Multicultural Perspectives* 13 (2): 79–89.

Yin, Hong-biao, and John Chi-Kin Lee. 2012. "Be Passionate, but Be Rational as Well: Emotional Rules for Chinese Teachers' Work." *Teaching and Teacher Education* 28 (1): 56–65.

Yorimitsu, Akiko, Stephen Houghton, and Myra Taylor. 2014. "Operating at the Margins While Seeking a Space in the Heart: The Daily Teaching Reality of Japanese High School Teachers Experiencing Workplace Stress/Anxiety." *Asia Pacific Education Review* 15 (3): 443–457.

You, Sukkyung, and Sharon Conley. 2014. "Workplace Predictors of Secondary School Teachers' Intention to Leave an Exploration of Career Stages." *Educational Management Administration & Leadership* 34 (4): 561–581.

Zeichner, Kenneth M., and H. G. Conklin. 2009. "Teacher Education Programs." In *Studying Teacher Education: The Report of the AERA Panel on Research and Teacher Education*, edited by Marilyn Cochran-Smith and Kenneth M. Zeichner, 645–736. Mahwah, NJ: Lawrence Erlbaum Associates.

Zigo, Diane. 2001. "Rethinking Reciprocity: Collaboration in Labor as a Path Toward Equalizing Power in Classroom Research." *International Journal of Qualitative Studies in Education* 14 (3): 351–365.

Index

Page numbers with *f* indicate a figure; page numbers with *t* indicate a table.

About the Authors

LYNNETTE MAWHINNEY is associate professor and chair of the Department of Curriculum and Instruction at the University of Illinois at Chicago. A former urban teacher of color herself, her work focuses on the professional lives of aspiring and current urban teachers and urban schooling. Dr. Mawhinney was awarded the prestigious Fulbright Core Scholar award in 2013. She has published extensively in both U.S. and internationally focused peer-reviewed journals. She is the author of *We Got Next: Urban Education and the Next Generation of Black Teachers* and co-editor of *Teacher Education across Minority-Serving Institutions: Programs, Policies, and Social Justice.*

CAROL R. RINKE is associate professor of education and assistant dean for Social and Behavioral Sciences at Marist College in New York. A former urban teacher, she returned to graduate school to study the challenges of recruiting and retaining educators in hard-to-staff classrooms. Her work focuses specifically on the intersection of the personal and the professional in teachers' career trajectories. Dr. Rinke is the author of over twenty publications on teacher career development that have appeared in journals such as *Teachers College Record, Teaching and Teacher Education*, and *Science Education.* She is also the author of *Why Half of Teachers Leave the Classroom: Understanding Recruitment and Retention in Today's Schools.*